Reading STREET

PreK-K

Scott Foresman

Read Aloud
Anthology

PEARSON Scott Foresman

Editorial Offices: Glenview, Illinois • Parsippany, New Jersey • New York, New York
Sales Offices: Needham, Massachusetts • Duluth, Georgia • Glenview, Illinois
Coppell, Texas • Sacramento, California • Mesa, Arizona

ISBN: 0-328-16174-8

1 2 3 4 5 6 7 8 9 10 V031 14 13 12 11 10 09 08 07 06 05

PreK Contents

Unit 1 All Together Now

Unit 2 Who Lives Here?

Unit 3 Watch Me Change

Unit 4 Let's Find Out

Unit 5 Going Places

Unit 6 Building Our Homes

Kindergarten Contents

Unit 1 All Together Now

Unit 2 Animals Live Here

Unit 3 Watch Me Change

Unit 4 Let's Explore

Unit 5 Going Places

Unit 6 Building Our Homes

Read Aloud Anthology

The Wheels on the Bus

ADAPTED BY JUDY AND DAVID GERSHON

The wheels on the bus go round and round,
round and round, round and round.
The wheels on the bus go round and round,
all through the town.

The wipers on the bus go swish, swish, swish;
swish, swish, swish; swish, swish, swish.
The wipers on the bus go swish, swish, swish,
all through the town.

The horn on the bus goes beep, beep, beep;
beep, beep, beep; beep, beep, beep.
The horn on the bus goes beep, beep, beep,
all through the town.

The door on the bus goes open and shut,
open and shut, open and shut.
The door on the bus goes open and shut,
all through the town.

The driver on the bus says "Move on back,
move on back, move on back."
The driver on the bus says "Move on back,"
all through the town.

The baby on the bus says "Wah, wah, wah;
wah, wah, wah; wah, wah, wah."
The baby on the bus says "Wah, wah, wah,"
all through the town.

The mommy on the bus says "Shush, shush, shush;
shush, shush, shush; shush, shush, shush."
The mommy on the bus says "Shush, shush, shush,"
all through the town.

The More We Get Together

ADAPTED FROM A TRADITIONAL RHYME

The more we get together
Together, together.
The more we get together
The happier we'll be!

For your friends are my friends
And my friends are your friends.
The more we get together
The happier we'll be.

The more we help each other
Each other, each other.
The more we help each other,
The happier we'll be!

I help you, you help me,
Yes, we help each other.
The more we help each other,
The happier we'll be.

We care for one another
Another, another.
When we care for one another,
The happier we'll be!

We're sharing and caring.
It's good to be sharing.
When we care for one another,
The happier we'll be.

The more we get together
Together, together.
The more we get together,
The happier we'll be!

For your friends are my friends,
And my friends are your friends.
The more we get together,
The happier we'll be.

Read Aloud Anthology

Music in the Night

By Etta Wilson

Oh, the moon came up one night
And set the big black dog to barking.
Bark Bark Bark

"Listen," said the cow.
"It's music in the night.
I'll sing too!"
Moo Moo Moo

Oh, the moon came up one night
And set the black dog to barking,
That set the cow to mooing.

"Listen," said the dove.
"It's music in the night.
I'll sing too!"
Coo Coo Coo

Oh, the moon came up one night
And set the big black dog to barking,
That set the cow to mooing,
That set the dove to cooing.

From *Music in the Night* by Etta Wilson. Text Copyright ©1993
by Etta Wilson. Reprinted by permission of Penguin Books USA.

© Pearson Education PreK

"Listen," said the hen.
"It's music in the night.
I'll sing too!"
Cluck Cluck Cluck

Oh, the moon came up one night
And set the big black dog to barking,
That set the cow to mooing,
That set the dove to cooing,
That set the hen to clucking.

"Listen," said the duck.
"It's music in the night.
I'll sing too!"
Quack Quack Quack

Oh, the moon came up one night
And set the big black dog to barking,
That set the cow to mooing,
That set the dove to cooing,
That set the hen to clucking,
That set the duck to quacking.

"Listen," said the horse.
"It's music in the night.
I'll sing too!"
Neigh Neigh Neigh

Read Aloud Anthology

Oh, the moon came up one night
And set the big black dog to barking,
That set the cow to mooing,
That set the dove to cooing,
That set the hen to clucking,
That set the duck to quacking,
That set the horse to neighing.

"Listen," said the cat.
"It's music in the night.
I'll sing too!"
Meow Meow Meow

Oh, the moon came up one night
And set the big black dog to barking,
That set the cow to mooing,
That set the dove to cooing,
That set the hen to clucking,
That set the duck to quacking,
That set the horse to neighing,
That set the cat to meowing.

"Listen," said the rooster.
"What's that awful
noise in the night?
I'll start my singing."
COCK-A-DOODLE-DO!

The sound of
the rooster's crowing
was the sign of
the night's going,
so as the moon went down,
the sun came up.
And that was the end of
music in the night!

The Lion and the Mouse

BY AESOP

EDITED BY LINDA YEATMAN

One day, a great big lion was sleeping in the sun. A tiny mouse scampered over him. The lion felt the mouse tickling him and he woke up.

"What do you think you're doing?" roared the lion. He put out his great big paw and trapped the little mouse.

"I did not mean to bother you," said the mouse. "I only wanted to be your friend. Please let me go free. If you do, I promise I will help you one day."

The lion laughed. "How could a tiny mouse like you help a great big lion like me?" he asked. But he let the little mouse go and went back to sleep.

Some time later, the lion was walking through the tall grass when he stepped in a trap that some hunters had set. The trap was made of strong ropes. As the lion struggled to get free, the ropes got tighter and tighter. Finally, the lion could fight no more. He lay on the ground, wrapped in the ropes, exhausted.

From *The Lion and the Mouse* by Aesop edited by Linda Yeatman, in Kindergarten Works. Published by Silver Burdett Ginn. Text Copyright © 1997 by Linda Yeatman. Reprinted by permission of Simon and Schuster.

Just then the lion felt a little tickle. It was the mouse, gnawing at the ropes. The little mouse chewed and chewed, and one by one, the ropes broke. Soon the lion was free.

"You really are a good friend," said the lion. "I didn't believe you could help me, but you did." And so saying, he scooped up the little mouse with his paw and set him on his shoulder. From that day on, the two friends were always together.

Colors

BY PAT O'KEEFE

We like many colors.
We see them with our eyes.
Yellow is the color
Of a shirt that's just my size!

We like many colors.
Yes, we see them with our eyes.
Your dog won a contest with a
Blue ribbon for first prize!

We like the different colors
Of balloons—red, white, and blue—
And flowers orange and purple
And pink and gold ones, too.

What color should we use now
To make a card for Gram?
I have my best green crayon.
Your favorite one is tan.

We can use both colors!
I'll draw a big green tree.
You'll draw Gram's tan house
On a card from you and me.

Gram will be so happy
When she sees what we have done.
She'll say, "I like both colors,
And two are better than one!"

Go Sleep in Your Own Bed

BY CANDACE FLEMING

Pig felt tired. It was time for bed. He headed to his sty, *joggety-jog*. But when Pig lay down, who do you think he found? It was Cow, sleeping soundly in the mud.

"Get up!" squealed Pig, shaking Cow wide-awake. "Go and sleep in your own bed!"

"So sorry," Cow yawned. "I didn't mean to sleep so long." And she headed to her stall, *clumpety-clump*. But when Cow lay down, who do you think she found? It was Hen, snoring loudly in the straw.

"Get up!" mooed Cow, shaking Hen wide-awake. "Go and sleep in your own bed!"

"Forgive me," Hen yawned. "I'll move quietly along." And she headed to her coop, *peckety-peck*. But when Hen lay down, who do you think she found? It was Dog, dreaming warm in the roost.

"Get up!" clucked Hen, shaking Dog wide-awake. "Go and sleep in your own bed!"

"Oops," Dog yawned. "O.K. Good-bye. I'm gone." And he headed for his kennel, *waggedy-wag*. But when Dog lay down, who do you think he found? It was Cat, napping cozy on the rug.

"Get up!" woofed Dog, shaking Cat wide-awake. "Go and sleep in you own bed!"

© Pearson Education PreK

"My mistake," Cat yawned. "Do forgive me, drooly one." And she headed to her loft, *pattery-pat*. But when Cat lay down, who do you think she found? It was the farmer, nodding off in the haystack.

"Get up!" mewed Cat, shaking the farmer wide-awake. "Go and sleep in your own bed!"

"Oh dear," the farmer yawned, "I've been napping way too long!" And she headed to her bed, *quickety-quick*. But when she lay down, who do you think she found?

"Surprise!" hollered Molly, popping out of the covers. "Do I have to go and sleep in my own bed?"

Said her mother with a smile, "Yes, we all need to sleep in our own beds."

Alice the Camel

Alice the camel has five humps.
Alice the camel has five humps.
Alice the camel has five humps.
So ride, Alice, ride.
Boom, boom, boom, boom!

Alice the camel has four humps.
Alice the camel has four humps.
Alice the camel has four humps.
So ride, Alice, ride.
Boom, boom, boom, boom!

Alice the camel has three humps.
Alice the camel has three humps.
Alice the camel has three humps.
So ride, Alice, ride.
Boom, boom, boom, boom!

Alice the camel has two humps.
Alice the camel has two humps.
Alice the camel has two humps.
So ride, Alice, ride.
Boom, boom, boom, boom!

Alice the camel has one hump.
Alice the camel has one hump.
Alice the camel has one hump.
So ride, Alice, ride.
Boom, boom, boom, boom!

Alice the camel has no humps.
Alice the camel has no humps.
Alice the camel has no humps.
'Cause Alice is a horse, of course.

Shopping Time

"Are you ready, Sarah?" Dad calls. "It's time to go shopping." Sarah comes quickly. She and Dad are going to the grocery store. Before they go, they take the time to make a shopping list. They write down milk, eggs, broccoli, and apples. It is a short list today!

At the store, Dad doesn't take a grocery cart. They can use a basket since he and Sarah only have four items to buy today. Sarah tries to remember what they are, but she knows her Dad has a list so they don't forget anything!

First stop is the produce section. Look at all the different colors! Here they find fresh vegetables and fruit. Sarah's favorite vegetable is broccoli. She says that it looks like little green trees. Sarah picks two big ones and puts them in the basket and asks, "What's next, Dad?"

"Since we are in the produce section, let's find the apples." her Dad replies.

Next to the vegetables is a big display of apples. There are so many different apples to choose from. Sarah sees red, pink, yellow, and green apples! Which should she choose? Sarah picks out yellow apples—she knows they are her Mom's favorite. Dad chooses some green apples that have a tart taste. "Green apples make my lips pucker, Daddy!" Sarah tells her Dad. They laugh and put the yellow and green apples into the basket. Sarah loves the colorful fruit section.

Next, they head for the dairy section. Here they can find items like milk, butter, cheese, eggs, and yogurt. Sarah and her dad have milk on their list so they get a gallon of milk and put it in their basket. Now they have three items in their basket. First, they found broccoli, then apples, and now milk. There is one more item on their shopping list. Sarah remembers! It is eggs! Let's find those eggs.

Since they are still in the dairy section, Sarah sees the eggs nearby. "Here they are, Dad! Let's put them in the basket."

Brrr! It's cold in this part of the store because of all the big refrigerators.

Sarah makes sure that they have forgotten nothing. Daddy and Sarah check their list.

"Let's see. Do we have broccoli?" Dad asks Sarah.

"Yes!"

"Apples?"

"Yes!"

"Milk?"

"Yes!"

"Eggs?"

"Yes!"

Now they have all four items checked off their list. Their basket is full, but Sarah and Dad have more to do at the store. They have to check out. They take everything from the basket and place it on the checkout counter. The cashier scans the items and then a bagger puts the items in bags. The cashier tells Dad how much everything costs.

Dad pays, and Dad and Sarah carry their groceries out to the car. Sarah helps Dad load the groceries in the car. At home, they unload the groceries and put everything away.

Grocery shopping is a lot of hard work, but Sarah is glad to help.

Read Aloud Anthology

Millie Wants to Play!

By Janet Pedersen

The barnyard was quiet and calm.

Millie opened her eyes. Everyone is still asleep and
I'm ready to play! Millie thought.

But Millie had to wait. She had to wait for the loud
rise-and-shine sound that meant time to play!

Just then, Millie heard
Baaaa! Ba-a-a-a! Baaaa!
That's not the rise-and-shine sound, Millie thought.

Too low and ripply. That sounds like . . . Lamb!
Lamb baaed and shook his woolly coat. But the others
were still asleep, so Millie waited.

Then Millie heard
Oink. Snuffle. Oink. Oink!
That's not the rise-and-shine sound, Millie thought.

Too deep and snorty. Sounds like . . . Pig!
Pig oinked and wiggled her snout in a greeting.
Millie swished her tail, but waited.

© Pearson Education PreK

Then Millie heard
Neigh! Ne-e-e-e-eigh! NEIGH!
That's not the rise-and-shine sound, Millie thought.

Too high and giggly. Sounds like . . . Pony!
Pony neighed and nodded good morning. Millie swished
her tail and stamped her hooves, but still she waited.

At last Millie heard a sound as loud as a trumpet.
It was the sound she'd been waiting for.
Cock-a-doodle doooooo!
The rise-and-shine sound! thought Millie.

Sounds like . . . Rooster!
The barnyard woke with sound as Rooster crowed
and flapped his wings.
Millie shook her ears, swished her tail, and stamped her
hooves. She could wait no longer . . . . Moooooooo!
Time to play!

Read Aloud Anthology

Watery World

"Hello, everybody! I'm Nancy, and I'm going to be your guide. Today we're going to see some creatures from the sea," says Nancy. Nancy is a diver at the aquarium, and she gets to be with the sea creatures each and every day.

Parents and children chatter noisily as they take their seats, but soon everyone quiets down. Their eyes are on Nancy. It's time for the show to start. It's time to watch. It's time to listen.

Nancy stands in front of an enormous tank of water. Inside it are two beluga whales splish-splashing around. These big white whales seem to be smiling as they swim back and forth. The thrilled audience "oohs" and "ahs," as they watch the lively whales leap above the water.

"The two swimmers behind me are Skip and Flip," says Nancy. "They are beluga whales. While they may look big to you, they are very small compared to other whales."

Nancy holds up a couple of fish and whistles to Skip and Flip. They leap from the water with their mouths wide open. Nancy feeds them the fish. In one gulp, Skip and Flip swallow the fish whole!

Nancy invites the audience to follow her. The next tank is much smaller, and it's swimming with color. Here tropical fish dart in and out of seaweed like flashing colored lights.

© Pearson Education PreK

"Look, that one is bright orange," someone cries.

"That fish has yellow stripes," says another.

"All these fish are from the ocean," says Nancy. "There they lived in coral reefs in warm water. As you can see, they come in many bright and beautiful colors!"

One little boy raises his hand to ask a question. "What is that bright orange and white fish?" he asks.

"That's a clown fish," Nancy answers. "And, right next to it is a seahorse, the creature with the curly tail. Has anyone ever seen a seahorse before?" All of the children shake their heads, no.

Another tank holds a few sea turtles. The green sea turtles have large feet that look like paddles and dark, hard shells. They swim up to the glass and stare at the children while the children stare back.

As they move to the next tank, one child shouts, "sharks." All the other kids run to see them. "This tank is home to hammerhead sharks," says Nancy as she prepares to feed them too. The circling sharks greedily go after the fish when Nancy drops them in the tank.

"Why do you think these are called hammerhead sharks?" asks Nancy. "Take one look at their heads, and you'll know why. Their flattened heads look like hammers! Notice how they go after the fish. That's just what they would do in the ocean!"

The tour with Nancy ends. The children have seen lots of sea creatures, but the sea is rich with life. Nancy has given them just a small peek into the wonderful watery world of the ocean.

Read Aloud Anthology

Bridget's Box

BY GINA CHESNES

Bridget watched the delivery people unload the new washing machine. She had never seen a box so large.

"Can I have that box?" she asked her daddy.

Daddy said, "Sure, you can have it. But what are you going to do with it? It's just a box."

Bridget patted the smooth cardboard. "Oh, I have big plans for this box," she said.

She dragged the box into her bedroom and shut the door. The box came up to the top of her head. She tipped it on its side, crawled inside, and curled up into a ball. She fit. It was warm and dark, like a cave.

Bridget climbed out and grabbed her blanket, her pillow, her rag doll, Lucy, and her brown crayon. She crawled back in and began coloring the inside of the box with her brown crayon. Now it looked like a cave. Bridget hid in the cave with Lucy until lunchtime.

"Having fun with your box?" Daddy asked at lunch.

"It's a cave," Bridget told him.

After lunch, Bridget went back to her cave. Now it felt dark and stuffy. Being in a cave all day was not much fun.

She sat down in front of the box. In one corner she put her doll bed. In the other corner, she put her doll table and chairs.

"Here you go, Lucy. Time to eat lunch," she said. She set Lucy on one of the chairs. Daddy peeked in the door.

"What a good idea for your box," he said.

© Pearson Education PreK

"It's a house for Lucy," Bridget told him.

"Emma is here to play with you," Daddy told her. Bridget's best friend, Emma, came in.

"What are you doing with that box?" Emma asked.

"It's a dollhouse," Bridget said.

They played dolls for a long time. After they put the dolls to bed, they didn't need a dollhouse anymore.

"Let's take the box outside," Bridget said. "It can be our car." The box banged into their legs and toes as they dragged it into the backyard. They both climbed in. They had to squeeze their knees to their chests to fit.

"We need a steering wheel," Emma said.

Bridget ran into the house and came back with a pie tin and tape. She taped the pie tin to the inside of the box.

"There's our steering wheel," she said.

Bridget and Emma took turns driving their car. They went to the park, to the grocery store, and to the circus. After the circus, Emma's mother came to pick her up.

"You sure are having a good time with that box," Emma's mother said.

"It's a car," they told her.

Soon it was Bridget's bedtime. As she climbed into bed, she heard the splatter of raindrops on her window. The box sat in the yard all night long. The next morning, when Bridget ran outside, her box was wet from the rain. It wasn't a car anymore.

Read Aloud Anthology

It was soft and leaned over. Bridget tried to climb in, but the box fell apart. She hung her head.

Daddy hugged her. "It was a very good box," he said.

"It was a cave and a dollhouse and a car," Bridget said sadly. "Now it's nothing."

Bridget plopped down on the steps while Daddy dragged the wet cardboard away. She missed her box.

Then she saw a delivery truck pull into her neighbor's driveway. Two men wheeled a huge carton inside. They came out with a large empty box. It was even taller than the washing machine box. This box was taller than the men!

Bridget hurried to the neighbor. "Can I have that box?" she asked him.

"I guess so, Bridget, but what are you going to do with it? It's just a box," said her neighbor.

Bridget smiled and patted the box. "Oh, I have big plans for this box," she said.

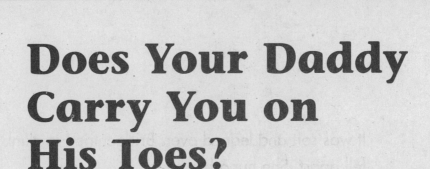

Does Your Daddy Carry You on His Toes?

BY BEVERLY STOWE MCCLURE

Does your daddy carry you on his toes?

A baby king penguin's daddy does.

After a mommy king penguin lays her egg, she goes to sea to find food. While she eats, the daddy carries the egg on his feet. When she returns, she carries the egg, and it's the daddy's turn to eat. A fold of skin on the parent's tummy covers the egg to keep it warm.

When the egg hatches, the mommy and daddy take turns carrying the downy soft chick on their feet until it grows too big.

Does your daddy carry you on his back?

A baby swan's daddy does.

A baby swan, or cygnet, climbs on its daddy's or mommy's back, sits between the wings, and hitches a ride across the water.

If a cygnet's brothers and sisters hop aboard, the ride can become quite crowded.

Does your daddy carry you in his mouth?

A baby Siamese fighting fish's daddy does.

A daddy builds a nest of bubbles in the underwater plants. A mommy lays her eggs, and the daddy catches

© Pearson Education PreK

them in his mouth. Then he puts the eggs in the nest and guards them until the babies hatch.

The baby fish, or fry, sometimes sink when they are learning to swim. The daddy gathers the fry in his mouth, then spits them to the surface so they can try again.

Does your daddy carry you in his pocket?

A baby sea horse's daddy does.

A mommy sea horse lays 200 eggs in the daddy's pouch on his tummy. He swims around the eggs until they hatch.

Baby sea horses are about the size of the nail on your little finger. They are so clear you can see right through them.

So if your daddy doesn't carry you on his toes, or on his back, or in his pocket, or in his mouth . . . where does he carry you?

He carries you in his arms, of course—the best place of all.

The Eensy-Weensy Spider

ADAPTED BY MARY ANN HOBERMAN

The eensy-weensy spider went up the waterspout.
Down came the rain and washed the spider out.
Out came the sun and dried up all the rain.
And the eensy-weensy spider went up the spout again.

The eensy-weensy spider got up one day in spring.
She stretched out all her legs and she began to sing.
"La!" sang the spider. "It's such a lovely day!"
And the eensy-weensy spider went skipping out to play.

The eensy-weensy spider met a baby bug.
"Hi!" said the spider and gave the bug a hug.
"Ugh!" said the bug. "Your hug is much too tight!"
"I'm sorry," said the spider. "I meant to be polite."

The eensy-weensy spider walked down the garden path.
Down came the rain and gave her quite a bath.
Out came the sun and dried her dry as chalk.
And the eensy-weensy spider continued on her walk.

The eensy-weensy spider went swimming to get cool.
"Out!" croaked the frog. "No spiders in my pool!"
"Please!" begged the spider. "I'd really like to swim."
So the frog allowed the spider to swim along with him.

The eensy-weensy spider had a heavy head.
"It's late!" said her mama. "Time to go to bed."
The spider was so tired she didn't make a peep,
And the eensy-weensy spider soon fell fast asleep.

The eensy-weensy spider slept right through the night.
When she awoke, the sun was shining bright.
"Good," said the spider, "there isn't any rain!"
And the eensy-weensy spider went up the spout again.

Special Day Routine

Each and every day Joshua gets up bright and early. The sun spills through his bedroom window, letting Joshua knows that it's time to start the day! Today Joshua yawns and stretches and then jumps out of bed. He's ready for the day! This is going to be a very exciting day.

First things first, Joshua toddles off to the bathroom to brush his teeth, wash his face, and comb his hair. He uses his blue toothbrush to clean his teeth. He likes the scrubbing sound the toothbrush makes against his teeth and the minty taste of the toothpaste. Sometimes when he's still sleepy, Joshua's eyes are half-closed as he brushes his teeth! Today that's not the case. Joshua is wide-awake! Today is going to be an exciting day for Joshua.

After brushing his teeth, Joshua washes his face with soap and water. He swishes and swirls the bar of soap around and around in his hands, making hundreds of tiny soap bubbles. Joshua slaps the soap on his face, being careful not to get it in his eyes. Soap stings! He rubs his cheeks, his chin, his nose, and a little bit behind his ears. He then rinses his face and uses a big, fluffy towel to dry it off. Then Joshua combs his hair. He doesn't want his hair to stick up today. Joshua checks himself out in the mirror. A clean, smiling face stares back at him.

"Joshua, your breakfast is almost ready. Hurry and get dressed. We don't want to be late today!" called Joshua's mother.

Joshua started to hurry. He hadn't even picked out his clothes yet! What would he wear today? Quickly, Joshua went into his closet and started looking around. Blue jeans? Yes. Should he wear the striped shirt or his favorite red shirt? Joshua finally chose his favorite red shirt. He was dressed for this special day.

Joshua's mom had breakfast ready. She had made a warm bowl of oatmeal, toast, a banana, and sweet orange juice for this special day.

"Thanks, Mom, for making my favorite breakfast," said Joshua. "How do I look? Do I look okay?"

"You look like you're going to have the best day ever," answered Joshua's mom.

Joshua smiled, but he had butterflies in his stomach! He was nervous about today. And, on top of his nervousness, Joshua still had a lot of things to do around the house before it was time to leave.

Every morning, Joshua helps clear the dishes off the table. He gives them to Mom. She puts them in the dishwasher. Joshua likes helping.

Then he runs upstairs to straighten his room. He makes his bed, smoothing the blankets and pillow. Joshua picks up any toys that he left out the night before and makes sure that everything else in his room is where it should be.

Now Joshua has brushed his teeth, washed his face, eaten breakfast, and finished his chores around the house. He has already done so much this morning, but he is sure that he will do even more during the day. Joshua picks up his backpack to get ready for the long and exciting day ahead of him. Yes, it's Joshua's very first day at school!

He peeks inside his backpack to make sure that everything is there. He has sharpened pencils in his pencil case. Joshua has red, blue, and yellow notebooks. He has a bright pink eraser. It makes a small thumping noise as it hits the bottom of the bag.

With everything in place, Joshua is ready for school! He puts his backpack on, holds Mom's hand, and sets off for school!

Annie's Wand

BY JENNIFER GROFF

Annie wanted to be a princess when she grew up. Alone in her room, she practiced. She put on her special princess dress. She stepped into her shiny princess shoes. And she placed her princess crown, glittering with jewels, on top of her head.

Then Annie walked like a princess over to her closet. She reached into the back and pulled her princess wand from its hiding place. Dancing like a princess, graceful and elegant, Annie smiled kindly at her court of dolls lined up to watch.

Annie didn't tell anyone about her plan to be a princess. She wanted it to be a surprise.

Sometimes Annie found it hard to keep her plan a secret.

When her brother Robert yelled, "Hey, frog face, what are you doing in there?" . . . Annie wanted to turn *him* into a frog.

When her father asked her, "Annie, have you set the table yet?" Annie wanted someone else to set the table.

And when her mother predicted, "Annie will definitely be a doctor or a firefighter when she grows up!" . . . Annie wanted to blurt out the truth. But she didn't.

One day, Annie went into her room for her princess rehearsal. She got out her princess dress and started putting it on over her clothes, but it was too tight.

Maybe if I take off my shirt, the dress will fit better, Annie thought. She had a hard time tugging off the dress.

Annie tried again, this time without her shirt underneath. The dress was still so tight she could barely breathe. As she yanked to pull it off, she heard the fabric rip.

"Oh no! My special dress is ruined! Well, at least I have my princess shoes," Annie said.

But Annie had to work to jam her foot into one shoe. When she tried the other, she couldn't even pull it over her heel. "This is worse than the glass slipper!" she wailed. "First my princess dress and now my princess shoes. Why is everything so small?"

Annie was afraid to try the princess crown, but she did. It teetered on the top of her head. Annie was so mad, she threw it across the room. As the crown rolled onto the floor, a precious jewel fell off and disappeared under the bed.

Annie started to cry. "How can I be a princess without my special dress and my shiny shoes and my jeweled crown? Why doesn't anything fit? It just isn't fair. I don't want to be just a frog-faced, table-setting firefighter!" She cried harder.

After a few minutes, Annie wiped her eyes with her torn dress. She looked at her dolls, waiting to watch the princess dance. It would be a shame to disappoint them.

Annie turned on the music. She started to dance, then stopped. Something was missing!

Annie walked, like a princess, over to her closet and reached into her secret hiding place. She pulled out the magic princess wand. Lightly she tapped herself on the head.

"I still have my magic wand," Annie said. "I can be whatever I want to be!"

And the princess danced, graceful and elegant, smiling kindly at her court of dolls lined up to watch.

Five Little Ducks

A TRADITIONAL RHYME

Five little ducks
Went out one day
Over the hill and far away
Mother duck said,
"Quack, quack, quack, quack."
But only four little ducks came back.

Four little ducks
Went out one day
Over the hill and far away
Mother duck said,
"Quack, quack, quack, quack."
But only three little ducks came back.

Three little ducks
Went out one day
Over the hill and far away
Mother duck said,
"Quack, quack, quack, quack."
But only two little ducks came back.

Two little ducks
Went out one day
Over the hill and far away
Mother duck said,
"Quack, quack, quack, quack."
But only one little duck came back.

One little duck
Went out one day
Over the hill and far away
Mother duck said,
"Quack, quack, quack, quack."
But none of the five little ducks came back.

Sad mother duck
Went out one day
Over the hill and far away
The sad mother duck said,
"Quack, quack, quack."
And all of the five little ducks came back.

A Picnic, Hurrah!

BY FRANZ BRANDENBERG

"Today is the picnic, hurrah!" exclaimed Elizabeth.

"It's our first picnic this year," said Mother.

"It's always nice to get together with friends," said Father.

All day Elizabeth and Edward planned the games. They were going to play catch-ball, horse and rider, and leapfrog. They were going to climb trees, hide in the bushes, and wade in the brook. Father went shopping. Mother prepared their favorite picnic food.

Finally it was time to go downstairs to meet their friends. Father carried the picnic basket. Mother carried the casserole. Edward carried the blanket. Elizabeth carried the ball. Just as they stepped outside, it began to rain. "Oh, no!" exclaimed Elizabeth.

"Oh, no!" shouted Edward.

"Oh, no!" said their friends Robert and Judith.

"We have looked forward to this picnic all week!" said Robert's and Judith's parents.

"What are we going to do?" asked Mother.

"We are going to have the picnic upstairs," replied Father.

"You can't have a picnic indoors!" said Edward.

"It's no fun to eat picnic food at the table!" said Elizabeth.

© Pearson Education PreK

"We were going to play catch-ball, horse and rider, and leapfrog," said Edward.

"We were going to climb trees, hide in the bushes, and wade in the brook," said Elizabeth.

"A picnic indoors is more fun than no picnic at all," said Mother.

Father pushed the table against the wall. Robert and Judith put the chairs on the table. Their parents rolled up the rug. Edward and Elizabeth spread the blanket on the floor. Mother handed out the paper plates. They sat by the baskets, and shared each other's picnic food.

Read Aloud Anthology

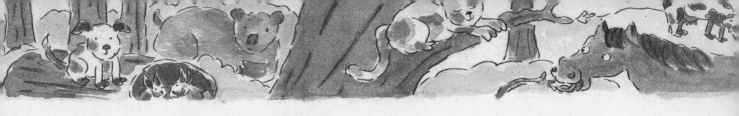

We're Going on a Bear Hunt

RETOLD BY MICHAEL ROSEN

We're going on a bear hunt.
We're going to catch a big one.
What a beautiful day!
We're not scared.

Oh-oh! Grass!
Long, wavy grass.
We can't go over it
We can't go under it.
Oh, no!
We've got to go through it!

Swishy swashy!
Swishy swashy!
Swishy swashy!

We're going on a bear hunt.
We're going to catch a big one.
What a beautiful day!
We're not scared.

© Pearson Education PreK

Oh-no! A river!

A deep, cold river.

We can't go over it

We can't go under it.

Oh, no!

We've got to go through it!

Splash splosh!

Splash splosh!

Splash splosh!

We're going on a bear hunt.

We're going to catch a big one.

What a beautiful day!

We're not scared.

Oh-oh! Mud!

Thick, oozy mud.

We can't go over it

We can't go under it.

Oh, no!

We've got to go through it!

Squelch squerch!

Squelch squerch!

Squelch squerch!

Read Aloud Anthology

We're going on a bear hunt.
We're going to catch a big one.
What a beautiful day!
We're not scared.

Oh-oh! A forest!
A big, dark forest.
We can't go over it.
We can't go under it.
Oh, no!
We've got to go through it!

Stumble trip!
Stumble trip!
Stumble trip!

We're going on a bear hunt.
We're going to catch a big one.
What a beautiful day!
We're not scared.

Oh-oh! A snowstorm!
A swirling, whirling snowstorm.
We can't go over it.
We can't go under it.
Oh, no!
We've got to go through it!

Hoooo woooo!
Hoooo woooo!
Hoooo woooo!

We're going on a bear hunt.
We're going to catch a big one.
What a beautiful day!
We're not scared.

Oh-oh! A cave!
A narrow, gloomy cave.
We can't go over it.
We can't go under it.
Oh, no!
We've got to go through it!

Tiptoe!
Tiptoe!
Tiptoe!
WHAT'S THAT?

One shiny wet nose!
Two big furry ears!
Two big googly eyes!
IT'S A BEAR!!!!

© Pearson Education PreK

Quick! Back through the cave! Tiptoe! Tiptoe! Tiptoe!

Quick! Back through the snowstorm! Hoooo woooo!
    Hoooo woooo!

Back through the forest! Stumble trip! Stumble trip!
    Stumble trip!

Back through the mud! Squelch squerch! Squelch squerch!

Back through the river! Splash splosh! Splash splosh!
    Splash splosh!

Back through the grass! Swishy swashy! Swishy swashy!

Get to our front door.

Open the door.

Up the stairs.

Oh, no!

We forgot to shut the door.

Back downstairs.

Shut the door.

Back upstairs.

Into the bedroom.

Into bed.

Under the covers.

We're not going on a bear hunt again.

Mary Wore Her Red Dress

Mary wore her red dress,
red dress, red dress,
Mary wore her red dress
all day long.

Kady wore her purple ribbons,
purple ribbons, purple ribbons,
Kady wore her purple ribbons
all day long.

Zak wore his green sweater,
green sweater, green sweater,
Zak wore his green sweater
all day long.

Toru wore his blue jeans,
blue jeans, blue jeans,
Toru wore his blue jeans
all day long.

Read Aloud Anthology

Sylvie wore her yellow pants,
yellow pants, yellow pants,
Sylvie wore her yellow pants
all day long.

Rico wore his brown sneakers,
brown sneakers, brown sneakers,
Rico wore his brown sneakers
all day long.

Larry wore his orange shirt,
orange shirt, orange shirt,
Larry wore his orange shirt
all day long.

The Cows on Uncle Eddy's Farm

BY JODI CHROMY

Tommy, Rachel, Danny, and Max were all playing hide-and-seek on Uncle Eddy's farm.

Tommy and Rachel were hiding.

Danny and Max looked all over the farm. They looked in the chicken coop. "Tommy, Rachel, are you in here?" called Danny and Max.

Cluck, cluck, cluck.

"They're not in here," said Danny.

"All that's in here are some chickens saying *cluck, cluck, cluck,*" said Max.

They looked in the pigpen. "Tommy, Rachel, are you in here?" called Danny and Max.

Oink, oink, oink.

"They're not in here," said Danny.

"All that's in here are some pigs saying *oink, oink, oink,*" said Max.

They looked in the hayloft. "Tommy, Rachel, are you in here?" called Danny and Max.

Meow, meow, meow.

"They're not in here," said Danny.

"All that's in here are some cats saying *meow, meow, meow,*" said Max.

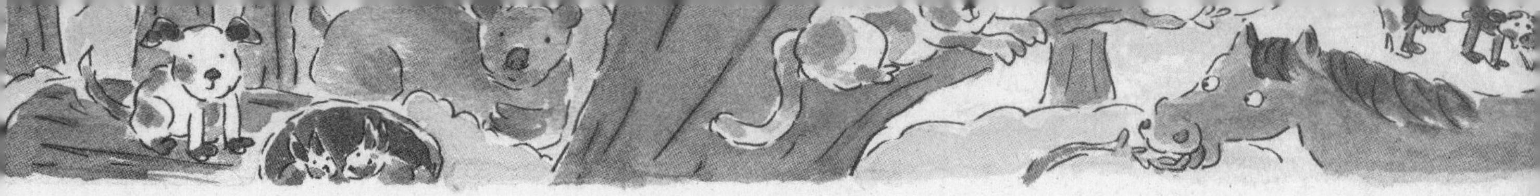

They looked in the pasture. "Tommy, Rachel, are you out here?" called Danny and Max.

Baa, baa, baa.

"They're not out here," said Danny.

"All that's out here are some sheep saying *baa, baa, baa,*" said Max.

They looked in the stable. "Tommy, Rachel, are you in here?" called Danny and Max.

Neigh, neigh, neigh.

"They're not in here," said Danny.

"All that's in here are some horses saying *neigh, neigh, neigh,*" said Max.

They looked in the barn. "Tommy, Rachel, are you in here?" called Danny and Max.

"No one in here but us cows!"

"They're not in here," said Danny.

"All that's in here are cows saying . . . *No one in here but us cows!*" said Max.

"How odd!" said Danny.

"Cows say *moo*!" said Max.

Danny and Max looked in the barn again. There were Tommy and Rachel, giggling, with the cows!

Teddy Bear, Teddy Bear

Teddy Bear, Teddy Bear, turn around.
Teddy Bear, Teddy Bear, touch the ground.
Teddy Bear, Teddy Bear, reach up high.
Teddy Bear, Teddy Bear, wink one eye.

Teddy Bear, Teddy Bear, slap your knees,
Teddy Bear, Teddy Bear, sit down please.
Teddy Bear, Teddy Bear, show your shoe.
Teddy Bear, Teddy Bear, that will do.

Teddy Bear, Teddy Bear, shut the door.
Teddy Bear, Teddy Bear, count to four.
Teddy Bear, Teddy Bear, go upstairs.
Teddy Bear, Teddy Bear, brush your hair.

Teddy Bear, Teddy Bear, turn out the light.
Teddy Bear, Teddy Bear, say good night.

Hey Diddle Diddle

Hey, diddle, diddle,
The cat and the fiddle,
The cow jumped over the moon.
The little dog laughed
To see such sport,
And the dish ran away with the spoon.

The Ants Go Marching

The ants go marching one by one.
Hoorah! Hoorah!
The ants go marching one by one.
Hoorah! Hoorah!
The ants go marching one by one;
The little one stops to suck his thumb,
And they all go marching down into the ground
To get out of the rain.
Boom, boom, boom, boom!

The ants go marching two by two.
Hoorah! Hoorah!
The ants go marching two by two.
Hoorah! Hoorah!
The ants go marching two by two;
The little one stops to tie his shoe,
And they all go marching down into the ground
To get out of the rain.
Boom, boom, boom, boom!

Read Aloud Anthology

The ants go marching three by three.
Hoorah! Hoorah!
The ants go marching three by three.
Hoorah! Hoorah!
The ants go marching three by three;
The little one stops to climb a tree,
And they all go marching down into the ground
To get out of the rain.
Boom, boom, boom, boom!

The ants go marching four by four.
Hoorah! Hoorah!
The ants go marching four by four.
Hoorah! Hoorah!
The ants go marching four by four;
The little one stops to shut the door,
And they all go marching down into the ground
To get out of the rain.
Boom, boom, boom, boom!

The ants go marching five by five.
Hoorah! Hoorah!
The ants go marching five by five.
Hoorah! Hoorah!
The ants go marching five by five;
The little one stops to take a dive,
And they all go marching down into the ground
To get out of the rain.
Boom, boom, boom, boom!

The ants go marching six by six.
Hoorah! Hoorah!
The ants go marching six by six.
Hoorah! Hoorah!
The ants go marching six by six;
The little one stops to pick up sticks,
And they all go marching down into the ground
To get out of the rain.
Boom, boom, boom, boom!

The ants go marching seven by seven.
Hoorah! Hoorah!
The ants go marching seven by seven.
Hoorah! Hoorah!
The ants go marching seven by seven;
The little one stops to count to eleven,
And they all go marching down into the ground
To get out of the rain.
Boom, boom, boom, boom!

The ants go marching eight by eight.
Hoorah! Hoorah!
The ants go marching eight by eight.
Hoorah! Hoorah!
The ants go marching eight by eight;
The little one stops to rollerskate,
And they all go marching down into the ground
To get out of the rain.
Boom, boom, boom, boom!

Read Aloud Anthology

The ants go marching nine by nine.
Hoorah! Hoorah!
The ants go marching nine by nine.
Hoorah! Hoorah!
The ants go marching nine by nine;
The little one stops to check the time,
And they all go marching down into the ground
To get out of the rain.
Boom, boom, boom, boom!

The ants go marching ten by ten.
Hoorah! Hoorah!
The ants go marching ten by ten.
Hoorah! Hoorah!
The ants go marching ten by ten;
The little one stops to shout
"THE END!!"

Windshield Wipers

BY DENNIS LEE

Windshield wipers
    Wipe away the rain,
    Please bring the sunshine
    Back again.
Windshield wipers
    Clean our car,
    The fields are green
    And we're traveling far.
My father's coat is warm.
    My mother's lap is deep.
    Windshield wipers,
    Carry me to sleep.
And when I wake,
    The sun will be
    A golden home
    Surrounding me;
But if that rain
    Gets worse instead,
    I want to sleep
    Till I'm in my bed.
Windshield wipers
    Wipe away the rain,
    Please bring sunshine
    Back again.

From *Alligator Pie* © 1977 by Dennis Lee. Reprinted with permission of Houghton Mifflin Publishing.

Down by the Station

BY LEE RICKS AND SLIM GAILLARD

Down by the station
Early in the morning
See the little pufferbellies
All in a row

See the station master
Turn the little handle
Puff, puff, toot, toot
Off we go!

Down by the station
Early in the morning
See the little pufferbellies
All in a row

See the station master
Turn the little handle
Puff, puff, toot, toot
Off we go!

My Cousin Katie

BY MICHAEL GARLAND

My cousin Katie lives on a farm. The big red barn is where the animals live. The little white house is where Katie lives. When the sun comes up, the rooster crows. Katie wakes up early. She helps her mother gather eggs for breakfast.

There are lots of animals on the farm. There are cows and goats and horses. There's a cat and a dog and a donkey named Margaret. Katie knows all about cows. They eat grass, make milk, and swat flies with their tails. The cat's name is Tiger. Tiger's job is to catch mice. On the farm there are fields of corn and lettuce. Katie wears a big hat when she helps to weed the lettuce patch.

The dusty, old tractor is very important. Katie's father uses it to plow the fields, spread seeds, and harvest the crops. When the tractor is broken, Katie helps her father fix it.

There is an apple orchard on the farm. When it is time to pick the apples, you fill basket after basket with big, red, juicy ones. In the meadow flowers grow wild. It's fun to gather great bunches of daisies, lilies, and goldenrod.

© Pearson Education PreK

Sometimes Katie and her mother have a picnic by the pond where the cows come to drink. When the sun goes down and the sky gets dark, the cows come home to sleep in the barn.

Tomorrow I am going to visit the farm. I can't wait to see all the animals, the apple trees, the meadow, and the big pond. but most of all, I can't wait to see my cousin Katie.

Ethan Wanted to Be a Backhoe

BY TRYN PAXTON

Ethan wanted to be a backhoe.

"Don't you mean you want to drive a backhoe?" asked his mom.

"No, I mean I want to *be* a backhoe," said Ethan.

Ethan asked Mom for a backhoe.

"But you already have a toy backhoe," said his mom.

"I want *two* so they can be friends," said Ethan.

When Ethan went to the library, he chose a book about backhoes.

"But you've checked out that book twice before," said his mom.

"This is the book I want," said Ethan.

One day a backhoe showed up at the construction site across the street from Ethan's house. Ethan sat outside the fence all morning and watched the backhoe work.

"Come home for lunch," Ethan's mom called.

"I'm not hungry," said Ethan. So Ethan's mom brought him a sandwich, and he ate while he watched the backhoe.

Later that afternoon Ethan's mom sat down next to Ethan and watched the backhoe with him. After a while she asked, "What would you do if you were a backhoe, Ethan?"

© Pearson Education PreK

"If I were a backhoe, I would dig in the dirt every day," said Ethan.

"Yes," said Ethan's mother. "A backhoe is a good digger."

"If I were a backhoe, I could live outside all the time," said Ethan.

"That's true," said his mother. "I don't think a backhoe would fit through the front door of our house."

"If I were a backhoe, I'd never have to brush my teeth," said Ethan.

"That backhoe's teeth do look pretty dirty," said Ethan's mother.

That night Ethan's mom tucked him into bed, straightened the covers, and turned out the light. When she kissed his forehead, Ethan said, "Mom, if I were a backhoe, would you still be my mom?"

"Yes," said Ethan's mom. "But I'd have a hard time getting my arms all the way around you to give you a hug."

"Then I guess you're glad I'm not a backhoe," said Ethan. And he hugged her back.

New School for Hopperville

Hopperville needs a new school. The architect has drawn plans for a school that will have two stories, a playground, and a parking lot.

A crane with a wrecking ball knocks down this old building to make room for the new school. Surveyors measure the ground to make sure the school is built in exactly the right place.

An excavator digs a large hole. Dump trucks take the dirt away. When the hole is done, workers dig a trench around the edges and line it with boards. A truck pours in concrete, which is very strong when it dries. The school will be built on the concrete foundation.

Trucks bring lots of steel beams. A crane lifts them into place and workers weld or bolt them together. Now there's a strong steel skeleton. It will hold up the walls and floors of the building—just like your bones hold you up!

A forklift carries the bricks to the bricklayers who are building the wall. They use a level to make sure the wall is straight.

The school looks done on the outside, but not yet on the inside. Electricians and plumbers put in wires and pipes. Concrete is poured to finish the floors. Carpenters build walls. Painters paint.

And, finally, one day, a school bus brings the children.

From *Click*, September 2003. Reprinted with permission of Carus Publishing.

© Pearson Education PreK

The Turnip

By Helen Oxenbury

Once there was a man who lived with his wife and little boy in a cottage in the country. One morning in May the man planted some turnip seeds.

Before long little turnip leaves began to poke up through the brown earth. Then an odd thing happened. One turnip plant began to grow faster than all the rest. It grew and it grew and it grew.

"We must have that turnip for supper tonight," said the man.

So he tried to pull the big turnip out of the ground. He pulled and he pulled and he pulled. But the turnip stuck fast.

"Wife, wife," he called, "come and help me pull this great turnip."

His wife came running. Then she pulled the man, and the man pulled the turnip. Oh how hard they pulled! But the turnip stuck fast.

"Son, son," called his mother, "come and help us pull this big turnip out of the ground."

The little boy came running and took tight hold of his mother. Then the boy pulled his mother, his mother pulled his father, and his father pulled the turnip. But still it stuck fast.

Then the little boy whistled for his dog.

"Come and help us," the boy said.

So the dog pulled the boy, the boy pulled his mother, his mother pulled his father, and his father pulled the turnip. But still it stuck fast.

Then the dog barked for the hen.

The hen came flying and grabbed tight hold of the dog's tail. Then she pulled the dog, the dog pulled the boy, the boy pulled his mother, his mother pulled his father, and his father pulled the turnip. But still the turnip stuck fast.

"Cluck, cluck, cluck!" cried the hen.

And the cock came flying to help. Then the cock pulled the hen, the hen pulled the dog, the dog pulled the boy, the boy pulled his mother, his mother pulled his father, and his father pulled the turnip and . . .

Whoosh! . . . Up came the turnip out of the ground, and down, backwards, they all tumbled in a heap. But they weren't hurt a bit and just got up laughing.

Then they rolled the turnip into the house and the boy's mother cooked it for their supper. Everyone had all they could eat and still there was enough left over for the next day, and the next, and the day after that!

The City Mouse and the Country Mouse

Once upon a time, a mouse who lived out in the country invited her old friend who lived in the city to come visit her. When the city mouse arrived, the country mouse tried very hard to make his visit a pleasant one. First they sat on the porch and listened to birds singing. Then she shared her simple dinner of bread and cheese with him.

The city mouse was not impressed. In fact he was bored. He told the country mouse, "Why, my dear, you must come visit me. I will show you what a wonderful life I have in the city. It is too quiet here for me. There is much more excitement where I live. And the food is so much better."

So the country mouse decided to go visit the city mouse's home. It was very noisy. Cars were honking and people were yelling. She was glad when they went inside. The people of the house had finished eating dinner and there were many wonderful things to eat still sitting on the table. What a feast! There was so much food—ham and potato salad and chocolate cake. The country mouse began to think her city friend was right and perhaps she should live in the city too. But just as the two of them were about to begin eating, they heard a terrible noise—loud, fierce barking was coming their way!

"Let's go," said the country mouse. "It's the dogs who live here. We'll have to hide for a while, but we can come back later."

The two of them scurried into a mouse hole where they stayed for a long time. Every so often a big, black nose sniffed at the hole. Finally, the dogs left and the city mouse suggested that they go back to the table.

The country mouse said, "You may like your exciting way of life, my friend. But I think I will go home now. It is better to have simple food in peace and safety than to have a feast in fear."

Read Aloud Anthology

Kindergarten Contents

Unit 1 All Together Now

Unit 2 Animals Live Here

Unit 3 Watch Me Change

Unit 4 Let's Explore

Unit 5 Going Places

Unit 6 Building Our Homes

Mary Had a Little Lamb

A CLASSIC NURSERY RHYME

Mary had a little lamb,
little lamb, little lamb.
Mary had a little lamb,
Its fleece was white as snow.

Everywhere that Mary went,
Mary went, Mary went.
Everywhere that Mary went,
The lamb was sure to go.

It followed her to school
one day,
school one day, school
one day.
It followed her to school
one day,
Which was against the rules.

It made the children laugh
and play,
laugh and play, laugh
and play.
It made the children laugh
and play,
To see a lamb at school.

And so the teacher turned
it out,
Turned it out, turned it out,
And so the teacher turned
it out,
But still it lingered near.

And waited patiently about,
Patiently about, patiently
about,
And waited patiently about
Till Mary did appear.

"Why does the lamb love
Mary so?
Love Mary so? Love
Mary so?"
"Why does the lamb love
Mary so?"
The eager children cry.

"Why, Mary loves the lamb,
you know.
Loves the lamb, you know,
loves the lamb, you know.
Why Mary loves the lamb,
you know,"
The teacher did reply.

Mr. Spuffington Fixes It Himself

BY JOHN GRANDITS

Mr. Spuffington's bathroom door won't close all the way. "Look, Pablo. It sticks because the top of the door is bumping."

"I'm very handy around the house," he tells Pablo. "I can fix that. If I hammer it down a little, the door will close again."

Mr. Spuffington gets out his stepstool and his hammer. He climbs up and gives the top of the door a little tap. *Tap, tap, tap.* That doesn't work. The door still sticks.

"I'll just hit it a little harder," he tells Pablo. *Bang! Bang!* The door still sticks.

Mr. Spuffington takes a great big swing. Oops! The hammer slips out of Mr. Spuffington's hand. It crashes down into the sink.

"Oh, no, Pablo. The faucet's broken and it's squirting water! I'm pretty handy, Pablo. But we'd better call Martin the Fix-It Man. QUICK!"

Martin the Fix-It Man gets there fast.

"No worries, Mr. S. I can fix it," says Martin. "First, let's turn off this water."

Martin reaches under the sink and twists a little handle. The water stops leaking.

"Mr. Spuffington Fixes It Himself" by John Grandits from *Click*, September 2003, Vol. 6, Issue 7.

"I'd better go get my tools. I have a new faucet in the truck," says Martin. Mr. Spuffington and Pablo start mopping up the water.

Martin takes a pipe wrench and unscrews the old faucet. Then he takes the new faucet and uses the wrench to attach it.

"I've got to make sure to tighten both the hot and cold water connections," says Martin. "And not too tight. They might break."

When Martin's done he turns the water back on.

"Wow," says Mr. Spuffington. "It works and no squirting!"

"How did the faucet break, Mr. S.?"

Mr. Spuffington explains about the sticking door and the hammer. He's a little embarrassed.

"No worries, Mr. S. I'll fix the door for you," says Martin.

Martin takes the pins out of the door hinges.

He takes down the door and stands it on its edge.

Then he takes out a tool and shaves little ribbons of wood off the end of the door.

"This is a plane," says Martin. "It's the perfect tool for a sticking door."

Then he lifts up the door and slides the pins back into the hinges. When they try the door it doesn't stick!

"Wow," says Mr. Spuffington.

"It opens and closes just like new."

"The next time you decide to fix something yourself, Mr. S., call me first," says Martin. "I'll get my tools ready."

Three Little Kittens

A CLASSIC NURSERY RHYME

Three little kittens,
They lost their mittens,
And they began to cry,
Oh, mother, dear,
We sadly fear,
Our mittens we have lost.

What! Lost your mittens,
You naughty kittens,
Then you shall have no pie.
Meow, meow,
Then you shall have no pie.

The three little kittens,
They found their mittens,
And they began to cry,
Oh, mother, dear,
See here, see here,
Our mittens we have found.

What, found your mittens,
You good little kittens,
Now you shall have
some pie.
Purr-rr, purr-rr,
Then you shall have
some pie.

Three little kittens,
Put on their mittens,
And soon ate up the pie.
Oh, mother, dear,
We sadly fear,
Our mittens we have soiled.

What! Soiled your mittens,
You naughty kittens,
And they began to sigh.
Meow, meow,
And they began to sigh.

The three little kittens,
They washed their mittens,
And hung them out to dry.
Oh, mother, dear,
Do you not hear,
Our mittens we have
washed?

What! Washed your
mittens?
You good little kittens!
But I smell a rat close by.
Meow, meow,
We smell a rat close by.

Freshly Baked

BY RON FRIDELL

Frank owns a bakery. He bakes all kinds of bread. He makes big loaves, small loaves, round ones, and square. He also makes dinner rolls and breadsticks and cookies and pies and doughnuts and bagels and cakes. But Frank can't make all these good things by himself. He needs help! He has people called bakers who help him. Each baker has a special job to do.

It's Leena's job to measure and mix the ingredients to make the bread dough. She measures flour, salt, sugar, shortening, yeast, and milk. Leena mixes the salt, sugar, and milk together. She heats the mixture on the stove until it's too hot to touch. Then Leena adds shortening. The shortening melts when it hits the hot milk. Next, it's time to add yeast. Yeast will make the bread dough swell up with air, like a balloon when you blow it up.

When Leena is done, Juan takes over. Juan puts the mixture into a big bowl. He uses a machine called a mixer to stir the ingredients together. As the mixer stirs, Juan adds flour, little by little. Now the mixture is called dough.

Soon the dough will be baked into bread. But first, strong hands must push and pull the dough to make it smooth and soft. That's Keisha's job. She plops the sticky dough onto a table and starts pushing and pulling it. She adds flour as she pushes and pulls. The flour keeps the dough from sticking to her hands. When Keisha is finished, the bread dough is a big, smooth, round ball.

Keisha puts the big ball of dough into a clean bowl. She lays a towel over the top and sets the bowl in a warm place in the kitchen. Now the yeast goes to work. It makes the dough swell up bigger and bigger. The dough rises up to almost twice its original size!

After the dough rises, Frank takes it from its warm spot. Today at the bakery they're making dinner rolls. Frank separates the big ball of dough into small balls. Each small ball will become a dinner roll. Frank puts flour on his hands as he works so the dough won't stick to his fingers. Frank places the rolls on baking trays and gives them time to rise some more.

Then it's Amanda's turn. Amanda must carefully slide each tray of dinner rolls into the hot oven. The oven bakes the dough until each ball has turned into a dinner roll. To make sure that the rolls don't bake for too long, Amanda sets a timer. When the timer rings, Amanda knows it's time to take the tray of rolls out of the oven. When the rolls are done, they have golden brown tops and smell warm and tasty.

As soon as the rolls are done, Frank sets them out to cool. Then he takes them from the kitchen to the store in front, where people can see them. Now customers can buy the freshly baked rolls. Some people will munch on the rolls at dinnertime. Other people will use them to make sandwiches for lunch. However people eat the rolls, they should all know that they were made by a team of bakers all working together. Without the work of Frank, Leena, Juan, Keisha, and Amanda, the bakery would have nothing to sell today! Each person helped make the rolls for the rest of us to eat and enjoy.

The Three Little Pigs

A TRADITIONAL TALE

Once upon a time there were three little pigs. Each little pig built a house for him to live in. The first little pig had built his house out of straw.

One day a wolf came to his door and said, "Little Pig, Little Pig, let me come in."

The first little pig replied, "Not by the hair of my chinny chin chin."

The wolf said, "Then I'll huff, and I'll puff, and I'll blow your house in."

The wolf huffed, and he puffed, and he blew the house in. The first little pig ran to the house of the second little pig. The second little pig had built his house out of twigs.

Along came the wolf. He said, "Little Pig, Little Pig, let me come in."

"Not by the hair of my chinny chin chin," said the second little pig.

"Then I'll huff, and I'll puff, and I'll blow your house in," said the wolf.

The wolf huffed, and he puffed, and he blew the house in. The first little pig and the second little pig ran to the house of the third little pig. The third little pig had built his house of bricks.

The wolf came to the brick house and said, "Little Pig, Little Pig, let me come in.

"Not by the hair of my chinny chin chin," said the third little pig.

Then I'll huff, and I'll puff, and I'll blow your house in," said the wolf.

Well, the wolf huffed, and he puffed, and he huffed, and he puffed, but he could not blow the house in. When he realized that after all his huffing and puffing and puffing and huffing, the house was still standing with the little pigs safe inside, he was very, very angry.

"I'm going to get you three little pigs," he shouted, "if it's the last thing I ever do!"

The wolf climbed up on the roof. He was going to come down the chimney into the house! But when the third little pig heard the wolf on the roof, he built a fire in the fireplace and put a big pot of water on the fire. Into the hot water fell the wolf and that was the last thing he ever did!

The Color Song

BY PAM SCHILLER

Red is the color for an apple to eat.
Red is the color for cherries too.
Red is the color for strawberries.
I like red, don't you?

Blue is the color for the big blue sky.
Blue is the color for baby things too.
Blue is the color of my sister's eyes.
I like blue, don't you?

Yellow is the color for the great big sun.
Yellow is the color for lemonade too.
Yellow is the color of a baby chick.
I like yellow, don't you?

"The Color Song" pp. 117–118 from *The Complete Book of Activities, Games, Stories, Props, Recipes and Dances for Young Children* (ISBN: 0-87659-280-9) by Pam Shiller and Jackie Silberg, are reprinted with permission from Gryphon House, PO Box 207, Beltsville, MD, 20704-0207. (800) 638-0928.

Green is the color for the leaves on the trees.
Green is the color for green peas too.
Green is the color of a watermelon.
I like green, don't you?

Orange is the color for oranges.
Orange is the color for carrots too.
Orange is the color of a jack-o'-lantern.
I like orange, don't you?

Purple is the color for a bunch of grapes.
Purple is the color for grape juice too.
Purple is the color for a violet.
I like purple, don't you?

Read Aloud Anthology

Baby Beluga

BY RAFFI AND DEBI PIKE

Actions Hands together, make the shape of a small whale jumping over the waves.

Baby Beluga in the deep blue sea,
Swim so wild and you swim so free.
Heaven above, and the sea below,
And a little white whale on the go.

Baby Beluga, baby Beluga,
Is the water warm? Is your mama home,
With you so happy.

Way down yonder where the dolphins play,
Where you dive and splash all day,
The waves roll in and the waves roll out.
See the water squirtin' out of your spout.

Baby Beluga, oh baby Beluga,
Sing your little song, sing for all your friends.
We like to hear you.

From *Raffi's Top Ten Songs to Read*. Copyright 1980, 1983 by Homeland Publishing, a division of Troubadour Records.

When it's dark, you're home and fed,
Curl up snug in your water bed.
Moon is shining and the stars are out,
Good night, little whale, goodnight.

Baby Beluga, oh baby Beluga,
With tomorrow's sun, another day's begun.
You'll soon be waking.

Baby beluga in the deep blue sea,
Swim so wild and you swim so free.
Heaven above and the sea below,
And a little white whale on the go.
You're just a little white whale on the go.

Read Aloud Anthology

The Mitten

A RUSSIAN FOLK TALE

It was a cold, cold day. A mouse was looking for a warm spot. Just then, the mouse saw something by a tree. It was a mitten, just one mitten.

"That looks like a good, warm home," the mouse said. "I'll just get in it to stay warm."

The mitten was just right for a mouse.

Then a rabbit came by. She was so cold. And the mitten looked warm.

"I'll just get in it to stay warm," said the rabbit.

"There is no room," said the mouse.

"I am so cold," said the rabbit.

"Well, maybe I can find a speck of room for you," said the mouse.

The rabbit got into the mitten. The mitten was getting a little crowded.

Then a fox came to the mitten. He was so cold. And the mitten looked warm.

"That looks like a good, warm home," the fox said. "I'll just climb in."

"There is no room!" said the rabbit.

"I am so cold," said the fox. "Please let me come in."

"All right," said the rabbit. "We'll squeeze together and make room for you."

The mouse and the rabbit squeezed together and the fox climbed in. The mitten stretched and stretched, but it managed to hold all three animals.

"The Mitten." Pearson Education.

"That's the last one!" squeaked the mouse.

Then a big bear lumbered up to the mitten. He was very, very cold, and the animals in the mitten looked so warm and cozy.

"That looks like a good, warm home," said the bear. "I'll just slip in and get warm."

"No room!" cried the fox.

"No room!" cried the rabbit.

"No room!" cried the mouse.

"Then make room!" cried the bear. "It's freezing out here!"

So the fox and the rabbit and the mouse all huddled very close together to make room for the bear. The bear pushed and squeezed himself into the mitten. The mitten stretched and stretched, but it didn't break.

Then a little cricket hopped up to the mitten. The poor little cricket was very, very cold. When she saw the mitten, she said, "That looks like a good, warm home. If I could just squeeze inside, I could get warm."

The mitten was already full with the mouse, the rabbit, the fox, and the bear, but the cricket was so tiny—surely there was room in the mitten for her.

Slowly she put one thin little leg into the mitten and when she did . . .

Rip! Rip, rip! And then . . . ka-boom!

The mitten burst apart. Pieces of mitten flew here, there, and everywhere! And out tumbled the bear, the fox, the rabbit, and the mouse.

The mouse looked at the rabbit. The rabbit looked at the fox. The fox looked at the bear. Then everyone looked at the cricket.

"Well, I guess I'll just be on my way," chirped the cricket. And away she hopped as fast as she could.

Read Aloud Anthology

All Night Near the Water

JIM ARNOSKY

In the golden glow of a summer evening, mother mallard leads her ducklings away from the nest in the tall meadow grass . . . to the lake.

The ducklings follow in a row around the shoreline weeds, through a driftwood maze, to a sandbar where they will spend their first night near the water.

Mother mallard tries to sleep but her ducklings are not sleepy.

They listen to the frogs, and spy on a heron catching fish.

The ducklings watch the dark shapes of bats flying in the twilight.

At nightfall the ducklings see lights twinkling over the water.

A hungry pike cruises by. Mother mallard calls softly for her ducklings to huddle near. She covers them with her wings and presses them against her sides.

Through the darkest hours of the night, mother mallard keeps her ducklings hidden, safe, and warm.

As the sun slowly rises, a sudden breeze ripples the lake.

When the world is light again, mother mallard flaps her wings and quacks out loud. Wake up! It's time to take a morning swim.

A new day has begun.

All Night Near the Water by Jim Arnosky. A Paper Star Book, Penguin Putnam Books for Young Readers, 1999.

How the Bear Lost Its Tail

ADAPTED FROM THE CLASSIC FOLK TALE

Once when winter was near, a hungry fox was searching for food. He saw strange animals on the riverbank.

"Those are otters!" he said. "They are the best meat in the world!"

He tried to catch the otters, but they saw him coming. They swam to their homes at the bottom of the river. Fox thought of a plan. He would catch the otters by fishing. His tail was long and bushy. But it was not long enough to reach the bottom of the river.

Fox went on his way. Soon he met Bear. Fox noticed Bear had a very long tail. Fox's eyes gleamed. "Oh, brother Bear," he said. "A big, strong animal like you should have the finest meat." He told Bear about the otters. "Let us work together to get the otters. We will have a feast!"

Bear smacked his lips. He followed Fox to the river. He bent over the water and saw his reflection. Bear thought it was an otter, so he pounced. The reflection went away. Bear waited. When the reflection came back, Bear pounced again.

"Brother Bear," said Fox, "that is the hard way to catch otters. Everyone knows you are a great fisherman. Fishing would be an easy way to catch them."

Bear was flattered. As Fox suggested, Bear swam to a log in the river. Then he dropped his tail into the water and waited. "When you catch an otter," said Fox, "toss it to the riverbank, and I will guard it for you."

The sun set, and Bear felt something bite his tail. He lifted it up. There was an otter! He swung his tail to toss it to shore. "Good!" Fox called. "Lower your tail again." Soon Bear had tossed many otters to the fox.

Bear was so intent on his fishing that he did not notice the sun had gone down. He did not hear the warning of the North Wind. He did not see the water turning to ice. Now he could not feel any biting at his tail.

"Fox," cried Bear, "what should I do?"

Fox said, "Wait! They will come back."

Night came, and Bear grew tired and hungry. "Brother Fox," he called, "let us go to my home and feast." There was no sound but the wind warning that winter had come. Bear tried to jump from the log, but his tail had become heavy. "Many otters!" he thought gleefully. He took a mighty leap and landed on the shore. "Strange," he said, "I feel so light!" He looked behind him. There were no otters. There was no tail! Fox was gone. All that remained of Bear's catch was a pile of bones.

Ever since, Bear has searched for his tail. But as hard as he looks, he cannot find it. To this day, Bear is still roaming the woods without a tail.

Willy's Winter Rest

By Donna Latham

Peeking from the tree trunk, Willy Dormouse blinked his big dark eyes and wriggled his tiny pink nose. He loved the smell of the meadow after a rainfall. Leaning out, Willy felt autumn's chilly wind ruffle his golden-brown fur. He flicked his silky tail and shivered. All the leaves were gone from the trees now. They rested in wet clumps beneath the tree trunk.

"Good evening, Willy!" called Mama Dormouse cheerfully. "Did you have a nice sleep? I love to snooze when it's raining, don't you?"

Willy yawned and stretched his tiny paws to the sky. "I'm still a little sleepy, Mama," he said.

"We'll take care of that!" laughed Papa Dormouse, calling from a stump across the way. He scurried down the stump, through the wet leaves, and up the tree trunk. He sat next to Willy.

"It's time for your first winter rest, my boy!" said Papa.

"Winter rest? What's that?" asked Willy. Willy had been born in the warmth of early June. His first summer was a delicious time! There were juicy berries to eat and crunchy nuts to snap between his little teeth.

During the hot summer days, Willy's family slept, safe and cozy in their nest in the tree trunk. Mama padded the nest with soft grass and bits of bark. Snuggled in the nest, Willy stayed away from the hawks that might scoop him up for lunch. He was safe from the snakes that slithered through the grass in search of a plump little dormouse.

© Pearson Education K

At night, Willy and his parents left the nest to search for food. Papa and Mama taught him how to scurry from tree to tree to tree without touching the ground.

"We can find yummy berries and nuts up here," explained Mama.

"Yes, and a crispy bug or two!" said Papa.

After summer came Willy's first autumn—a flurry of activity! His parents were so busy. First, Papa had searched for a perfect winter place. Deep down, at the bottom of the tree trunk, Papa found just the right spot. Warm, safe, and tucked away, it would become a winter hideaway.

Next, Mama made a nest there, fluffing it with grass. She nibbled away chips of bark from the trees outside and placed them, just so, in the nest to build a winter bed.

"Are we going to sleep here now?" asked Willy, looking eagerly at the cozy bed.

"No, not just yet," said Mama.

Then, during their midnight hunts for food, Willy, Mama, and Papa brought extra food back to the tree trunk. Papa showed Willy how to stash the food near the winter bed.

"Why are we stashing food?" asked Willy.

"Well," explained Papa, "We're going to sleep for a long time—til April! On warm winter days, we might wake up. If we do, you can bet we'll be hungry. So we'll have a snack before we settle back to sleep."

"Speaking of eating," called Mama from above, "It's time for dinner!"

Willy and Papa scurried up the tree trunk. Willy blinked his black eyes in surprise at the huge feast Mama had spread out.

"Now, Willy," said Mama. "It's time to fatten up! Our bodies need enough food for those long, long months when we're asleep."

"That's right," said Papa. "We need to get twice as big as we are now."

"Wow!" said Willy. "Pass the berries, please!"

Willy munched and crunched. He gobbled grains and nibbled nuts. Soon, Willy was stuffed.

"Oh, my!" he squealed. "I've never felt so full in my whole life." He patted his bulging tummy.

"Good job!" said Papa Dormouse. "Now remember, if you wake up on a warm day, there will be plenty to eat. It's waiting for you."

"I don't think I'll ever eat again," said Willy.

"Oh, just wait!" laughed Mama. "There's nothing like a winter rest to work up an appetite."

Willy yawned. He stretched his tiny paws and flicked his long tail.

"I'm so tired!" he said, blinking his black eyes. "I can barely keep my eyes open."

"It sounds like you're all set for winter," said Papa. "It's time to settle in."

Finally, with their bellies full, the family scampered down to their winter bed. Willy looked around at the soft nest. He saw the food they had stocked in case they woke up on warm days. He felt cozy and safe.

"Now, Willy," said Mama, "Roll yourself up into a tight little ball."

Willy ducked his head down and tucked his paws close to his body. He wrapped his long silky tail around himself.

"Perfect!" said Mama, as she patted soft grass around him. "Good night, sleep tight! See you in the spring!"

"Or on a warm day!" said Papa.

But Willy couldn't answer. Snug in the winter bed, he was already asleep.

The Ants and the Grasshopper

BY AESOP

One beautiful spring day, a grasshopper was hopping about making music. He came upon some ants busily working in their garden. The grasshopper played his music and danced, but the ants kept on hoeing and planting seeds.

"Why are you working so hard on such a fine day?" asked the grasshopper. "Come and have fun. This is a time for music."

Without stopping a moment to rest, the ants explained that they had jobs to do. They were planting a garden so they would have food for the winter.

"That's silly," said the grasshopper. "There's plenty to eat." And he pointed to the green leaves and the grass and the flowers blooming everywhere.

"Warm weather doesn't last forever," said the ants, and they continued to work.

The grasshopper laughed and twirled around and went back to playing.

Spring turned to summer. While the grasshopper lay in the shade without a care in the world, the ants tended their garden in the hot sun. They watered the plants, pulled out the weeds, and raked the soil. They picked ripe fruits and vegetables.

Fall came, and in the chilly air the grasshopper still amused himself with his own music. The ants harvested their crops and stored them in the tunnels of their ant hill.

Winter howled and snow covered the ground. Inside the ant hill, the ants were warm and had plenty of food. Outside in the icy wind, the grasshopper wandered about searching for leaves and blades of grass, but he found nothing. He was cold and hungry and frightened.

One day, thin and shivering, the grasshopper knocked at the ants' door. "Who's there?" called the ants.

"It is I, Grasshopper," the grasshopper answered in a weak, small voice.

When the ants opened the door, the grasshopper said meekly, "I'm cold and hungry. May I come in and have something to eat?"

The ants looked at him. All through the spring and summer and fall, while they had worked and worked, the grasshopper had done nothing but dance and play. Now he was paying for his foolishness, but the ants could not help but feel sorry for him. Finally one ant said, "We will be glad to let you in, if you promise to help us in our garden next spring."

"I will help you work," promised the grasshopper. "Please, let me spend the winter here."

All winter long, the grasshopper lived comfortable with the ants who had stored enough food to last the winter. And when spring came, the grasshopper kept his promise. All day long, he worked in the ants' garden. Sometimes at night, after the digging was done and the ants were at rest, he would make music. He had learned that it is best to work first and play when the work is done.

Anna Panda Trades Places

BY RON FRIDELL

Anna Panda woke up one morning and looked in the mirror. She saw a furry white face with black ears, a black nose, and big black rings around her eyes. When Anna smiled, her eyes sparkled, just like her mother's. Today, Anna Panda was going to do something she had never done before.

"That's right," she said to her face in the mirror. "I, Anna Panda, am going to trade places with my mother."

Mama Panda was at the kitchen counter making Anna's lunch. Anna pulled one of Mama Panda's aprons from a drawer and tied the apron strings tight around her waist. Now Anna Panda looked just like Mama Panda, only shorter. Anna had to stand on a chair to reach the counter beside her mother.

"I will finish," Anna said.

A very surprised Mama Panda watched as Anna finished making her school lunch and putting it in a brown paper bag. Then Anna used a marker to write a name on the bag in big purple letters and handed the bag to her mother. The name on the bag was MAMA PANDA.

"And what is this?" Mama Panda asked.

"It's your lunch, Mama. We're trading places. I am staying here just like you, and you are going to school just like me."

"You are playing a joke on me, Anna," Mama Panda laughed. "Right?"

But Anna Panda shook her head no. "While you are at school, I will do the dishes and wash the clothes and sweep the floors," Anna said. "And when you get home from school, I will make a snack of milk and cookies for you."

"Ah," said Mama Panda. "And then what?"

"Then you will go out to play nicely with the other children until I call you in for dinner," Anna said.

"That is very silly," Mama Panda said. But then she thought a moment and took off her apron. "All right, let's give it a try. I will help you get started before I leave for school."

Anna was so excited as Mama Panda handed her the broom and dustpan. Now she, Anna, was the grown-up. But Anna had a very hard time with the broom. The handle was so long that she kept banging it into things.

"Oh, sweeping is much harder than I thought," Anna said. "I will skip the sweeping for now."

So Mama Panda took Anna to the laundry room with the great big washing machine and dryer. Mama pointed to a heaping basket of dirty clothes. The basket was taller than Anna. "Oh dear," Anna said. "It will take me all day to get these clothes all washed."

"And then you must get them dried," Mama Panda said. "And then you must fold them. And then you must put them away."

"Oh," Anna said with a great big gulp. "Oh, dear."

"So, you better get started right away."

Anna followed Mama into the kitchen. "Well, I'm off to school," Mama said, grabbing the brown paper bag with MAMA PANDA written on it. "Where I can learn new things and play with all my friends—and eat this delicious lunch my mama made for me."

"Oh no you don't," Anna said, and grabbed the lunch from her mother. Anna crossed out MAMA and wrote ANNA on the bag.

"So," Mama Panda said. "I am the grown-up and you are child again?"

"Oh yes," Anna said. "I like it so much better this way."

"Me too," Mama Panda said.

And Anna Panda gave Mama Panda a great big hug.

"There's the bus, better hurry," Mama said.

Mama Panda watched as the school bus pulled up and Anna got on. Then the bus pulled away, and Mama Panda put her apron back on with a great big smile.

The Ugly Duckling

ADAPTED FROM THE CLASSIC TALE

Once upon a time, a mother duck sat on her nest, busily hatching her ducklings. One by one the eggs cracked open, and little ducklings stuck their heads out of the shells and said, "Quack, quack, quack." Soon all but the biggest egg had hatched.

At last the big egg cracked open. "Cheep, cheep!" said the youngster as he scrambled out of the egg. He was so big and so ugly that the mother duck looked and looked at him. "A turkey egg must have gotten into my nest by mistake," said the mother duck. "I will find out if he is a turkey." She led her ducklings into the water. They all began to swim, and the Ugly Duckling was the best swimmer of all. So the mother duck knew this ugly bird was not a turkey.

After the swim, the mother duck took her new family to the barnyard. All the animals came to see the ducklings. When they saw the Ugly Duckling, they made fun of him and called him names.

The Ugly Duckling was so miserable that he scrambled over the fence and left the barnyard. He ran and ran until he came to a marsh. There he met some wild geese, who said he could fly south with them. The Ugly Duckling was about to agree when some hunters came and the wild geese quickly flew away.

The Ugly Duckling hurried over fields and meadows until he came to an old house. He squeezed through a crack in the door and went in. An old woman lived there with her cat and her hen. "Well, you certainly are an ugly bird," the old woman

said, "but if you lay eggs, you can stay." After a week, the Ugly Duckling had laid no eggs, so the old woman told the poor bird to leave.

Winter was coming and the Ugly Duckling tried to stay warm. One night as he slept on a pond, the water froze all around him, and he was trapped in the ice. A farmer found and freed the bird. He took the Ugly Duckling home with him. The farmer's children began chasing the Ugly Duckling. The Ugly Duckling dashed out of the house, glad to be free again.

During the long winter, the Ugly Duckling suffered. But when the sun began to shine warmly, he knew spring was on the way. He spread his wings and began to fly until at last he came to a lovely garden that had a flowing stream.

He flew down to the stream and was resting on the water when he saw three beautiful white swans swimming nearby. The Ugly Duckling was so unhappy and lonely that he decided to take a chance.

"I will swim near those royal birds. Perhaps they won't mind."

So he swam toward the swans. When they saw him, they hurried toward him. "Please let me stay," he said, and he bowed his head.

As he bowed his head, he looked down into the water and saw himself. "What is this?" he exclaimed. "I am no longer an ugly gray bird. I am a beautiful swan!

The other swans swam around him and stroked him with their beaks to greet him. The Ugly Duckling was filled with happiness. The bird that had been so mistreated because of his ugliness was now the most beautiful of all birds—a swan.

The Knee-High Man

AFRICAN FOLK TALE BY JULIUS LESTER

Once upon a time there was a knee-high man. He was no taller than a person's knees. Because he was so short, he was very unhappy. He wanted to be big like everybody else.

One day he decided to ask the biggest animal he could find how he could get big. So he went to see Mr. Horse. "Mr. Horse, how can I get big like you?"

Mr. Horse said, "Well, eat a whole lot of corn. Then run around a lot. After a while you'll be as big as me."

The knee-high man did just that. He ate so much corn that his stomach hurt. Then he ran and ran and ran until his legs hurt. But he didn't get any bigger. So he decided that Mr. Horse had told him something wrong. He decided to go ask Mr. Bull.

"Mr. Bull? How can I get big like you?"

Mr. Bull said, "Eat a whole lot of grass. Then bellow and bellow as loud as you can. The first thing you know, you'll be as big as me."

So the knee-high man ate a whole field of grass. That made his stomach hurt. He bellowed and bellowed and bellowed all day and all night. That made his throat hurt. But he didn't get any bigger. So he decided that Mr. Bull was all wrong too.

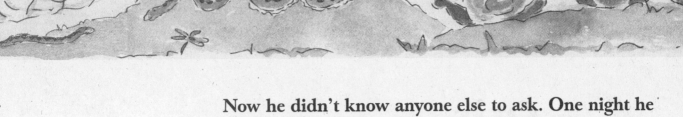

Now he didn't know anyone else to ask. One night he heard Mr. Hoot Owl hooting, and he remembered that Mr. Owl knew everything. "Mr. Owl? How can I get big like Mr. Horse and Mr. Bull?"

"What do you want to be big for?" Mr. Hoot Owl asked.

"I want to be big so that when I get into a fight, I can whip everybody," the knee-high man said.

Mr. Hoot Owl hooted. "Anybody ever try to pick a fight with you?"

The knee-high man thought a minute. "Well, now that you mention it, nobody ever did try to start a fight with me."

Mr. Owl said, "Well, you don't have any reason to fight. Therefore, you don't have any reason to be bigger than you are."

"But, Mr. Owl," the knee-high man said, "I want to be big so I can see far into the distance."

Mr. Hoot Owl hooted. "If you climb a tall tree, you can see into the distance from the top."

The knee-high man was quiet for a minute. "Well, I hadn't thought of that."

Mr. Hoot Owl hooted again. "And that's what's wrong, Mr. Knee-High Man. You hadn't done any thinking at all. I'm smaller than you, and you don't see me worrying about being big. Mr. Knee-High Man, you wanted something that you didn't need."

Otis

BY JANIE BYNUM

Otis was a very fine pig. He had soft, silky hairs and pink, pink skin. How such a neat pig was born to such a sloppy family was anyone's guess. When his brothers played rugby in the swamp, Otis kept score on the sidelines. When his sisters played tag in the wallow, Otis counted buttercups in the grass. Otis tried very hard to remain a spotless pig.

But making friends wasn't easy.

His mama told him, "Someday, Otis, you will like the mud."

And Otis replied, "Oh Mama, I don't think so."

Otis imagined mud oozing around his hooves, making a sticky, sucking noise as he lifted one foot, then the other. He imagined mud drying on his skin, leaving dirty patches all over his pink, pink body.

Even when he did his chores, Otis managed to stay clean. While his brothers weeded the corn, Otis hauled the weeds away, careful not to get a spot of mud on his pink, pink self. While his sisters picked the ripe corn, Otis sorted the good ears from the bad, making sure not a bit of dirt soiled him.

Otis was lonely. All the other pigs loved mud. But no matter how hard he tried, he just couldn't stand the stuff.

His papa told him, "Someday, Otis, you will like the mud."

And Otis replied, "Oh, Papa, I don't think so."

One day as Otis returned from the garden, he heard a small, croaky sob. There by the wallow sat a little frog, crying softly.

"Little Frog, why are you crying?" Otis asked.

"I've lost my favorite ball in the middle of the mud," Little Frog said.

"Well, that's not so bad. Go get it," Otis said.

"But I can't cross the mud!" Little Frog wailed.

"Why not?" Otis asked. "Frogs love mud and all things swampy."

"Not this frog!" Little Frog cried. "Please wade in and get my ball," he begged. "Pigs love mud and all things sloppy."

"Not this pig!" Otis replied.

Little Frog stopped crying, and croaked a little laugh. Otis oinked a little giggle.

"I have an idea," Otis said. "I'll hold on to this branch, and you can hop out to get your ball."

"That's a fine idea," Little Frog said.

And that is what they did.

The rest of the afternoon, Otis and Little Frog tossed the ball back and forth on the nice, clean grass. And from that day on, the two friends played together everywhere— except, of course. . . in the mud.

Daisy's Seeds

BY DONNA LATHAM

"Come on, Daisy!" Grandpa Jack called. "It's a big day—planting day."

Daisy jumped for joy. She had been waiting for this day. She plopped on her floppy straw hat and stepped into her shiny gardening boots. Every spring since Daisy had been tiny, she had helped Grandpa Jack plant his spring garden. Now, in the yard, they dug in.

They first cleared away dried leaves and twigs. Then, using a hoe, Grandpa Jack dug long rows in the dirt. As Grandpa Jack worked the soil, Daisy watched wriggling worms. She smelled the heavy scent of earth.

Soon, it was time for Daisy's favorite part. Walking along the straight, neat rows, careful not to step on them, she sprinkled seeds.

As Daisy drizzled seeds into place, Grandpa Jack covered them with dirt. Then he marked the rows with little signs. On each was the name of the flower that would spring to life in the ground.

"We're growing flowers from A to Z and all the colors you can imagine," chuckled Grandpa Jack. "Asters, bright purple, will shoot up here," he said. He marked the row with a sign that said "Asters."

"Purple asters," Daisy sighed.

"Grandma's favorites are next," said Grandpa Jack, sticking another sign in the black dirt. "Baby's breath, white as snow. Then cosmos, yellow as the sun."

"White baby's breath, yellow cosmos," Daisy said. If she closed her eyes, she could practically smell them.

Daisy and Grandpa Jack worked their way through the rows. Four o'clocks, poppies, snapdragons, zinnias. Daisy repeated the flowers' names. They tickled her tongue and made her smile.

"This year, we'll try something special," said Grandpa Jack, as they moved to a sunny part of the yard.

"We'll plant seeds just for you. You can take good care of them and watch your flowers grow."

"Yippee!" cried Daisy. "My own flowers!"

"Scooch down low," said Grandpa Jack. From his overalls pocket, he removed a little shovel.

"First, dig a nice, warm bed for your seeds."

Carefully, Daisy dug. Grandpa Jack handed her a fistful of seeds. Daisy placed them into the dirt.

"Now, tuck them in with a blanket of soil," said Grandpa Jack. "Just like I tuck you in at night!"

Finally, they were finished. Grandpa Jack pushed back his cap and mopped his face with his handkerchief. Smiling, he wiped a blotch of dirt from Daisy's cheek.

"Let's give all our seeds a good soaking," he said.

Using the hose, Grandpa Jack filled Daisy's sprinkling can. Daisy watered her seeds, while Grandpa Jack soaked the rest.

"We've given our seeds a drink. Now, it's time to let the sun do its work!" said Grandpa Jack. "Speaking of drinks, isn't it time for us to go inside for lemonade?"

The next day, Daisy raced home from school to check her flowerbed. Her little brother, Leo, was squatting beside it.

"I think these seeds are broken," he said. "I don't see anything."

Daisy smiled. "They're sleeping in the dirt," she said. "Pretty soon they'll peek out."

"When?" asked Leo.

Grandpa Jack joined them. "It takes light, water, and time for seeds to grow. Now step back, please, and give these seeds some light!"

Leo and Daisy laughed.

Over the next three days, the sun shone brightly. Each day, Daisy checked her flowerbed. There was no sign of life. Wasn't the sun doing its job?

On the fourth day, a giant rumble rocked the house. Thunder woke everyone up like a noisy alarm clock.

Daisy ran from her bed. She met Leo and Grandpa Jack at the front window. They loved to watch the rain.

"Are the seeds going to drown?" asked Leo.

"Oh, no!" smiled Grandpa Jack. "You wait and see...."

The next day, the sun returned to its place high above the garden. In no time, the yard was dry. As usual, Daisy dashed to her flowerbed.

"Grandpa Jack!" she called. "Come quick!"

Tiny, perfect leaves of green were peeking through the earth.

"Oh, Grandpa Jack, what will they be?" asked Daisy, as Grandpa Jack squatted beside her.

Pulling a little sign from his overalls pocket, Grandpa Jack marked the flowerbed. "My favorite flowers in the world—daisies!" he said.

Color Me Chameleon

BY COLLEEN SPAETH

If I were a chameleon, and not a kid, I'd use my strong hands to climb in trees and stay there ALL day. I could reach the highest branches and not fall off once. No homework for me! I would live in a beautiful rainforest. And all that rain wouldn't bother me--not one bit.

If I were a chameleon and came to school, at recess I'd be the hide-and-seek champion! No one would ever find me. I'd change color from my hair to my shoelaces to match my hiding spot. If I were hiding in a tree, I'd be tree-colored. If I were hiding in a chair, I'd be chair-colored. If I were hiding next to a wall, I'd look just like the bricks! Those other kids could look and look but in my hiding spot I'd be almost invisible. If I were a chameleon.

If I were a chameleon, I would have eyes that move in two directions at once! Imagine that! My right eye looking up, my left eye looking down. One eye looking forward and one eye looking behind me (just in case my little sister tried to sneak up on me). Yes, how handy to have those special eyes. I could do twice as much as regular people can. I could read a book while watching a movie! My parents would be so proud!

If I were a chameleon, I would eat bugs and slugs. (That's what chameleons eat, you know.) My tongue would be very long and so sticky those bugs wouldn't have a chance to escape. Zap! My tongue would be lightning fast. Crunch! I'd eat all those bugs for lunch.

But yuck! Who wants to eat all those slimy slugs and crunchy bug? Could my chameleon tongue catch some cereal and sandwiches? How about apples and cookies? Those are the foods I like to eat. I guess for now I won't be a chameleon. I'll keep my two eyes facing front. I'll stay me-colored and never get to be tree-colored. And I will not eat bugs.

But still, wouldn't life be fun—if I were a chameleon?

A Day Like Every Other Day

BY RON FRIDELL

Most days are a lot alike. I do the same things in the same order, from when I wake up with the sun in the morning to when I go to sleep at night with the moon. But each day is different too. Like today.

Today I wake up bright and early, like always. I see the Sun coming up outside my window and I say, "Hello, Sun!" Then I jump out of bed and wash my face, just like I do every morning.

Now it's time to get dressed for school. What will I wear today? How about my brand new orange and black shirt that makes me look like a tiger? That is something different.

Then I hurry downstairs to help Mom make my lunch. We make a peanut butter and honey sandwich and put carrot sticks in a little plastic bag. Then Mom surprises me with a fruitcup for my lunch. Now that is different too!

Now it's time for breakfast. Most days I have crunchy cereal, but today Dad makes fluffy pancakes. That is something different! While we eat Dad's fluffy pancakes, we laugh and talk, just like we always do.

Every day Mom and Dad walk me to school. Today, Maria, Nicholas, and Anthony are walking with their parents too, so we all walk together. Sometimes we must hurry to keep from being late. But today we have lots of time. So we all stop to watch a family of ducks paddling around in the river. "Quack, quack," we call to them. That is something different! When we get to school, Mom and Dad give me a quick little kiss on the cheek, like always.

Today our teacher, Mrs. Jacobs, introduces us to the letter *M*. She has us think of *M* words, like *marker* and *map* and my favorite *M* word—*mom*! It's easy for Maria to think of an *M* word. Her name starts with *M*! We learn about letters every day, but each day it's a new letter. And that is something different!

At the end of the school day, Mom waits for me outside the school's front door, like always. "We have to make one stop on the way home," Mom says. We take the bus to the big bookstore to get a gift for Grandfather. "Pick out a book for us to read at bedtime too," Mom says. Now that is something new and different!

Mom and Dad make dinner and I set the table, just like every night. Tonight Dad makes his special chili. Dad hardly ever makes chili, so this is something different! We eat every last bite. Then we all help clear the table and do the dishes, just like every other night.

After dinner, I take a bath. Then it's time for bed. Mom tucks me in, just like every night. "This has been a very fun day." I say. "I did so many different things."

"And tomorrow will be a day just like it," Mom says as she turns off the light. Together, we wave to the moon in the window and say, "Goodnight moon," like always.

As I fall asleep I think of all the new and different things I did today. What new and different things did you do today?

The Three Billy Goats Gruff

A NORWEGIAN TALE RETOLD BY HUGH LUPTON

Once upon a time there were three Billy Goats Gruff and they were making a journey to the green hill where the grass grows thickest and sweetest. On their way they came to a high bridge over a deep river. Under that bridge there lived a knobbledy troll, as old and as cold as a boulder of stone.

First of all came the youngest Billy Goat Gruff, lifting up his hooves and trip-trap, trip-trap, trip-trapping over the bridge. The troll's ears twitched, his nose wrinkled and his mouth opened. "WHO'S THAT trip-trapping over my bridge?"

"It's only me, the littlest Billy Goat Gruff. I'm going to the green hill to eat and eat and make myself fat."

The troll licked his gray lips with his red tongue. "I'm coming to gobble you up!"

"Oh no, Mr. Troll, I'm much too small. Why don't you wait for the second Billy Goat Gruff? He's far bigger than me."

"Very well," grunted the troll. "Away with you!"

So off he trotted, and soon he was nibbling the thick, sweet grass on the green hill.

A little while later came the second Billy Goat Gruff, lifting up his hooves and TRIP-TRAP, TRIP-TRAP, TRIP-TRAPPING over the bridge. The troll's ears twitched, his nose wrinkled and his mouth opened. "WHO'S THAT trip-trapping over my bridge?"

"It's only me, the middle sized Billy Goat Gruff. I'm going to the green hill to eat and eat and make myself fat.

"The Three Billy Goats Gruff" from *The Story Tree Tales to Read Aloud*, first published in 2001 by Barefoot Books. Text copyright © 2001 Hugh Lupton. Reprinted by permission.

The troll licked his gray lips with his red tongue. "I'm coming to gobble you up!"

"Oh no, Mr. Troll, I'm much too small. Why don't you wait for the third Billy Goat Gruff? He's far bigger than me."

"Very well," grunted the troll. "Away with you!"

So off he trotted, and soon he was nibbling the thick, sweet grass on the green hill.

A little while later came the third Billy Goat Gruff, lifting up his hooves and TRIP-TRAP, TRIP-TRAP, TRIP-TRAPPING over the bridge. The troll's ears twitched, his nose wrinkled and his mouth opened. "WHO'S THAT trip-trapping over my bridge?"

"It's only me, the biggest Billy Goat Gruff. I'm going to the green hill to eat and eat and make myself fat."

The troll licked his gray lips with his red tongue. "I'm coming to gobble you up!"

But the biggest Billy Goat Gruff lowered his head and said,

"Come along, Mr. Troll, and gobble your fill.
I've got two horns, as sharp as thorns,
That'll toss you over the hill."

And when the troll came clambering up over the side of the bridge, the Billy Goat charged and caught him on the sharp prongs of his horns and tossed his head so that the troll was thrown high up into the sky and then hard down on the ground far beyond the green hill. And that was the end of him.

And as for the three Billy Goats Gruff—if they aren't fat yet, then they're munching still at the thick, sweet grass on the green hill. And that was the end of that story.

The Tale of Peter Rabbit

ADAPTED FROM THE CLASSIC TALE

Once upon a time there were four little rabbits. Their names were Flopsy, Mopsy, Cottontail, and Peter. They lived with their mother under the roots of a big tree. One day, Mrs. Rabbit was going to town. She warned the four little rabbits, "You may play in the fields or run through the woods, but don't go into Mr. McGregor's garden." Then Mrs. Rabbit went to town to buy a loaf of bread and five blackberry muffins.

Flopsy, Mopsy, and Cottontail were good little rabbits and went to play in the woods. But Peter didn't listen to his mother. He went right over to Mr. McGregor's garden and squeezed under the gate. He ran through the garden, eating all the lettuce, beans, and carrots he could find. He began to get a stomachache, so he went to look for some parsley to chew. He stepped around the corner and almost ran into Mr. McGregor, who was on his hands and knees planting cabbage. He jumped up and began chasing Peter with his rake, yelling, "Stop, you thief!"

Scared for his life, Peter ran all over the garden looking for the way out. He lost one of his shoes in the cabbage patch and one in the potato plants. Then he ran into a strawberry net and got caught by the large buttons on his jacket. He heard Mr. McGregor coming, so he wiggled out of the net, leaving his jacket behind. He ran to the tool shed and hid in a watering can. He heard Mr. McGregor come into the tool shed. Suddenly Peter sneezed. Mr. McGregor tried to grab Peter, but he jumped out of the watering can and through a small window.

Finally, Mr. McGregor got tired of chasing Peter and went back to planting cabbages. After wandering through the garden for a long time, Peter finally found the way out. He ran lickity-split as fast as he could past Mr. McGregor and slipped safely toward the gate and headed toward home.

Mr. McGregor hung Peter's jacket and shoes on a scarecrow to frighten the birds and to warn other little rabbits not to come into his garden.

Peter was so tired that when he finally got home he flopped down on the floor of the warm kitchen and shut his eyes. He was not feeling very well. Mrs. Rabbit gave Peter some medicine and sent him straight to bed without any supper.

But Flopsy, Mopsy, and Cottontail, who had been good little rabbits, had bread and milk and blackberry muffins for supper.

A Canary's Song

BY TIMOTHY B. COLLINS

One night while Huey was trying to sleep, his new canary started singing in its cage. *Cheep cheep cheep!*

Huey tossed and turned for almost an hour before he finally fell asleep.

The next morning he asked his new pet, "Why did you keep me awake last night with your singing?"

"It's cold in my cage at night," the canary said. "You have covers on your bed, and I have nothing to keep the chill out of my cage."

That night, before Huey went to bed, he placed one of his dad's shirts over the canary's cage to keep the night air out. All was quiet for a short while, and then the canary started singing again. *Cheep cheep cheep!*

"What's wrong?" Huey asked.

"It's lonely in here," the canary said. "I'm used to having other birds in my cage to keep me company."

The next day, Huey found a mirror and placed it inside the cage with the canary. "There," Huey said. "Now when you feel lonely, just look into the mirror and you will see another bird in there with you." The canary thanked Huey for the mirror. He sat looking at himself for a long time.

That night, Huey was almost asleep when the canary started singing again. *Cheep cheep cheep!*

"What now?" Huey asked.

"I miss my swing," the canary said. "I used to have a swinging perch to rock myself to sleep."

Huey promised that he would go to the pet store the next day and buy a swinging perch for his pet canary.

The next night, Huey placed the swinging perch in the cage.

"Now you can rock yourself to sleep," Huey said. "And maybe I can get some sleep."

Huey lay in his bed for a while, waiting for the canary to sing. All was quiet. No singing. Huey rolled over. "Finally," he said, "a night of good sleep."

Several minutes passed by. Huey rolled back over to his other side. He couldn't sleep. It was too quiet.

"Canary bird," Huey said as he sat up in bed.

"Yes?" the canary said.

"I can't sleep," Huey said. "Could you sing me a lullaby?"

"I would love to," the canary said.

The canary started singing a soft, sweet song. *Tweet tweet tweet.*

Soon Huey was fast asleep.

Peggy Penguin Goes to the Ocean

By Colleen Spaeth

Far away on the bottom of the world lived a young penguin chick named Peggy. She loved her cold, wintery home. She loved cuddling with the grown-up penguins as the freezing winds blew. She loved the snow piled up into a white hill of snow. And she especially loved playing with her penguin friends. Every day Peggy and her penguin friends waddled up their hill of snow. One by one they slid down the hill beak-first. *What fun!* thought Peggy.

The day finally came that the grown-up penguins gathered the little penguin chicks to make their first long trip to the ocean. These penguin chicks were growing up fast and had to learn how to catch their own food. Peggy looked back at the white hill of snow where she always played. *Good-bye, snow hill!* she thought. *See you soon!*

Together all the penguins started the journey. They waddled for a long time. Sometimes, they waddled up hills. Sometimes, they slid down beak-first. *Just like on the snow hill at home!* Peggy thought happily. Finally they reached the ocean.

Peggy looked out at the ocean. It was shining in the cold sun. It looked big!

Peggy waddled along the shore marveling at the water's soft, splashy waves. She came across a huge rock, taller and wider than her. She touched the rock with her flipper. It was soft. She tapped it with her beak. It made a barking sound.

"Hey, you there," barked the rock, "stop poking me!"

"Who are you?" squeaked Peggy.

The rock moved and turned a large head towards the little penguin. "Haven't you ever met a seal before?" asked the rock that was really a seal.

"No, I haven't," said Peggy, "You're the first one I've ever seen." She looked at the seal. It had a round nose with long whiskers and beautiful black eyes.

The seal lifted a heavy flipper and pointed at the shore behind him. There were hundreds of seals lying among the rocks.

"We're all seals here on this beach," said the seal, "You're a penguin and everyone knows that penguins don't belong here. You should go back to your friends."

Peggy said a quick good-bye and waddled as fast as her feet could go, back to her friends. *Wait 'til they hear about the seals!* she thought.

There was no time to tell them, though. As soon as Peggy got back to her friends, it was time for her to learn how to swim and catch food. The penguin chicks lined up and one by one, they dove beak-first into the water. Peggy took a big breath and dove into the ocean with a splash! She opened her eyes. The world under the water was amazing! She could see the other penguins above and below her swimming in every direction. Peggy did an underwater spin. She pushed herself forward and kicked with her feet. She zipped through the water. *Whee!* thought Peggy.

She looked for the other penguins. They were catching small fish and shrimp called *krill* in their beaks. Peggy tried it. The krill were delicious, but she had trouble catching the small fish—they were fast!

Peggy swam back to her friends. She could see them playing by the shore, jumping in and then out of the water. She couldn't wait to tell them about her exciting day!

Apple Juice Tea

BY MARTHA WESTON

Polly has a mama, a daddy, and a gran. Polly's gran lives far away. Now she is coming to visit.

"You were a tiny baby the last time you saw Gran," says Mama. "Do you remember her?"

Polly sees Gran's picture in the hall every day. She thinks she remembers Gran a little bit.

Gran comes on a big plane. Mama says it's Gran, and Daddy says it's Gran, but her face doesn't look like her picture in the hall.

"I have a hug for you, Polly," says Gran. But Polly doesn't know Gran, and she doesn't want Gran to hug her.

At home, Polly wants to be with Mama, but Mama is always talking to Gran.

At the zoo, Gran says, "Will you show me the gorillas, Polly?"

"I always see gorillas with Daddy," says Polly.

At the park, Gran says, "Want a push on the swing, Polly?"

"Mama always pushes me on the swing," says Polly.

At bedtime, Daddy says, "Let Gran read you *The Three Bears,* Polly."

"No!" says Polly, "I don't want a story."

She wishes it could be Polly and Mama and Daddy and that's all. But the next morning when Polly gets up, Gran is still there.

Apple Juice Tea by Martha Weston. © 1994 by Martha Weston. Published by Clarion Books. Reprinted by permission of Houghton Mifflin Co.

Gran has made buttery, warm biscuits. Polly is eating one when Mama says, "Polly, Daddy and I are going out tonight, and Gran is going to baby-sit you."

"But Ellie is my baby-sitter," says Polly. "I want Ellie to come."

"Ellie is busy and Gran wants to help. I'm sure you'll have a good time," says Mama.

"We could have a tea party tonight, Polly," says Gran.

"No we couldn't," says Polly.

"Why not?" asks Mama.

"Pretty Doll and Mr. Bun always spill their tea," says Polly.

"How about if you and I have apple juice tea and Mr. Bun and Pretty Doll have macaroni tea?" asks Gran.

"Maybe," says Polly.

After supper it's time to hug Mama and Daddy goodbye. Polly holds on tight. Then she runs to her room and shuts the door. She doesn't want Gran to help her put on her pajamas.

After a while, Gran peeks in. "I don't want a tea party," says Polly.

"Okay," says Gran. "What *do* you want to do, Polly?"

Polly looks out the winow. It is starting to get dark. She hears crickets. "I want to take Pretty Doll and Mr. Bun for a walk," she says. She is sure Gran will say, "Not now, honey, it's bedtime."

But Gran says, "Okay."

"Really?" Polly can't believe it. "In my pajamas?"

"Sure," says Gran.

Polly gets her slippers and puts Mr. Bun and Pretty Doll in her old stroller. "I'm going to the corner. I'll be back soon," she tells Gran.

Polly starts walking down the sidewalk. Soon she comes to the bump in the cement where she tripped once and skinned her knee. She wants to show this to Gran. Polly calls to Gran, "You come too, okay?"

Gran joins her. Polly shows Gran the sidewalk bump. She shows her the blackberry bushes and the neighbor's cat.

It is a warm night. They walk up to the corner and back down, talking the whole time.

Back on her doorstep, Polly has an idea. "Wait!" she tells Gran. "I will go in first. Then you knock. You are my visitor."

Polly goes inside and shuts the door. Soon there is a knock. "Who is it?" calls Polly.

"It's Gran. I've come to visit you," Gran calls back.

Polly opens the door. "Okay, come in! Would you like some tea?" Gran has a big smile. "Oh, yes I would, thank you," she says.

They go into the kitchen. Polly gets a big tray and Gran puts apple juice, cups, and saucers on it. Polly pours dry macaroni into little cups for Mr. Bun and Pretty Doll.

Gran starts to put the tray on the big table.

"Yoo-hoo, Gran!" says Polly. "I'm down here! Let's have tea in my table house."

So Gran and Polly have an apple juice tea party under the big table. Polly decides she likes the way Gran holds her cup and saucer. She tries to hold hers the same way.

It is past Polly's bedtime when she crawls under the covers and listens to Gran read *The Three Little Pigs*. Gran has a funny, squeaky pig voice and a deep, growly wolf voice. Then Gran sings a lullaby that Polly has never heard before. It is a long one, a little sweet and a little sad. While Gran is singing, Polly falls asleep.

The next morning, Gran is still there. Polly and Gran go to the store together to buy more apple juice.

The Naughty Shoes

MODERN DUTCH FOLK TALE BY PAUL BIEGEL

Have you ever crawled into bed at night with your shoes on? Of course not! You take them off and put them under your chair or under your bed. Grown-ups do the same thing. So just imagine how many thousands of pairs of shoes stand under beds and chairs during the long, dark night, while their owners lie under the covers asleep.

Do the shoes also sleep? Heavens no! Shoes never get tired. Listen to this:

One night my father's left shoe said to my father's right shoe, "I am sick and tired of taking Father places; all day long I have to go where he wants to go—this way and that way, up way and down way, in way and out way! Now I am going by myself, and I am going the *other* way!"

"I am going with you," said my father's right shoe.

So off they went through the open window, out into the dark street. It sounded like a man walking in the street, but it was only an empty pair of shoes, going the other way.

"Coming along?" they called through the open window to the neighbors' shoes. And the shoes of the neighbor—husband and wife—joined my father's shoes; their neighbors' shoes came along too, and the shoes of the neighbors of the neighbors, all down the block.

It became quite a parade. Clickety-click went the high heels; boom-boom went the heavy boots; schwee-schwee went the rubbers. Shoes, shoes, and more shoes—old pairs,

From *The Naughty Shoes* by Paul Biegel, translated by Celia Amidon.
Reprinted by permission of *Cricket Magazine*, December 1974.
Copyright © by Paul Biegel.

worn-out pairs; shiny shoes, unpolished shoes, scuffed shoes; brown ones, black ones, big ones, small ones. They walked, they ran, they skipped—always the other way, for this was the Free Shoes Parade and their owners' feet were all at home under the covers.

"Left belongs to right!" called the shoes. "Hold on to each other by the laces!"

But Grandma's left shoes lost track of Grandma's right shoes. And the shoes without laces couldn't hold on to each other at all.

"Where are you? Where are you?" voices called out in the dark.

"I'm here! I'm here!" came the answers from here and there and everywhere.

But which belonged to which? There was too much confusion for the right shoes to find their lefts and for the lefts to find their rights.

"Never mind," someone shouted. "Every shoe for himself from now on. We don't need to be paired off."

And off they went again. Single left shoes and unmatched right shoes. Hoppety-hop. The very dainty and the very shiny shoes waded through all the mud puddles, what fun! But the old, scuffed shoes, the dirty and unkempt ones, walked primly with neat little steps and avoided the puddles. The shoes of old people hopped, skipped, and jumped. The children's shoes took slow, dignified steps. Shoes without feet cramped inside them. Shoes who were their own masters. They all had a glorious time, a wonderful, marvelous time!

"We have to go home! We have to get back before our people get out of bed!" shouted the shoes, and the jolly parade changed into a scramble of confusion and panic.

Most of the shoes had lost their way and did not know how to get home. As the sun rose higher in the sky, they stampeded through the streets, clickety-click, boom-boom, schwee-schwee, scuff-scuff. Boots stomped over slippers. Shoes tripped over their untied laces. Toe-caps banged against toe-caps, and heels stepped on toes.

The sun climbed higher and higher.

"Hurry, hurry!" shouted the shoes. "We'll be late! Quick, get inside!"

Most of the shoes climbed inside the first open window they saw and settled under the first bed they could find. Two left men's shoes under Grandma's bed. Wading boots under the bed of the two-year-old Caroline. And when my father got up, he found under his bed a lady's pump, a blue sneaker, a left slipper, and a right boy's shoe.

"What in the world . . ." said my father.

"What in the world . . ." said all the people in town when they got out of bed. And that morning a parade of limping people went to work and to school, for they were all wearing the wrong shoes. Either too big or too small. Either two right shoes or two left ones—click-scuff, boom-schwee, schwee-click. Grandma went around in stocking feet, and Caroline went barefoot.

Everyone asked, "Who has my shoes? Who's wearing my shoes?" And everyone examined everyone else's feet. Now and then someone shouted "Ah! There's my brown right shoe!" Or, "Yoo-hoo, you have my red sandal!"

And so, slowly but surely, everyone got his own shoes
back again.

It took longer for my father, though, than for anyone
else. Because his left shoe had climbed a tree, and it was
not until three days later that the wind finally blew
it down.

The Mysteries of Flight

BY JENNIE SPRAY DOERING

Maria Alvarez woke up in the middle of the night knowing she could fly. She drifted up off her bed and began swimming through the air. She twirled to the ceiling. She swooped, she loop-de-looped, she floated on her back. When she got tired, she sank smoothly back down to her bed.

The next morning, when she tried to tell people, no one believed her.

When she tried to prove it to them, she discovered they were right.

She *couldn't* fly. She could run and jump. Leap from her bed. Dive from the playground swing set. But nothing worked.

Sometimes, it seemed the more people watched, the harder she fell.

After a while, she gave up even trying.

Then one cool and lonely night, Maria made up her mind to try one last time. Maybe she could only fly at night? Maybe she could only fly when no one was looking? She didn't know. She just wanted to fly again, more than anything.

And suddenly, she was.

Maria didn't waste any time worrying about who was watching or what they might think. She angled herself through the window, out into the night. In some places, the air felt bumpy and knocked her about. The wind blew her hair into her face, but she took no notice.

"The Mysteries of Flight," by Jennie Spray Doering. Reprinted by permission of *Ladybug* magazine, January 2004, Vol. 14, Issue 5. Copyright © by Jennie Spray Doering.

She flew—over dusty rooftops, through damp, misty clouds, and into a glittering sky. She tumbled with stars and hummed lullabies with the moon until her whole body was tired.

She drifted down, slipped back through her window, and gently curled up in her own warm bed.

That morning she untangled one tiny moonbeam, still glowing, from her hair. But she didn't tell anyone.

Maria knows she may never understand all the mysteries of flight. But she still keeps on practicing. Because someday, she might.

Read Aloud Anthology

Ready for a Ride!

Sari and Grandma love going for bicycle rides. It's their favorite thing to do on bright, sunny days. They ride all over the neighborhood. But before Sari and Grandma can take a bike ride, they have to get ready.

First, Sari and Grandma check their bicycles. Everything has to be working right to have a safe bike ride. Grandma checks the bicycle tires to make sure they have the right amount of air in them. She sees that the front tire of Sari's bike is a little flat. That can make a bike very hard to ride! So Sari and Grandma grab their bicycle pump. A pump pushes air into a tire to fill it up. *Whoosh, whoosh, whoosh.* Grandma checks the tire again. Now it's just right for a ride.

They check all the chains too. The chains connect the pedals and the wheels. Without the chains, those bikes couldn't go anywhere. Grandma gives Sari a thumbs-up sign. The chains are in good shape. They move well. Those bikes are ready to go!

Now Sari and Grandma must think about other ways to stay safe. Sari knows that bike riding is fun, but it is easy to get hurt if you fall down. That is why she and Grandma have safety gear to wear when they go out on their bikes.

First Sari and Grandma put on their kneepads. Kneepads fasten around the legs. They are soft on the side by your knee and hard on the outside. If a bike rider falls, kneepads protect the knees from scrapes or injuries. Sari and Grandma put on elbow pads too. Just like kneepads, they keep you from hurting your arms in case of falls. Sari and Grandma know that it's important to protect the

elbows and knees. Even though neither of them has ever fallen, they wear kneepads and elbow pads every time they ride.

The most important thing to wear when riding a bike is a helmet. Your head contains your brain, which controls everything your body does. Bumping your head during a fall can be very dangerous. Bike helmets help protect the head. They are made of hard plastic and they have a special lining that keeps the impact, or hard bump, from hurting your head. Helmets have straps that fasten underneath the chin and keep them on a bike rider's head. Sari's bright pink helmet is smaller than Grandma's. It fits her just right, and it helps drivers to see Sari so that they don't get too close to her. It wouldn't be safe for Sari to wear Grandma's helmet because it might not stay on Sari's head if she fell. Sari and Grandma strap on their helmets. Grandma makes sure Sari's chin strap is snug.

With tires pumped, knee and elbow pads on, and helmets in place, Sari and Grandma are ready for their Saturday afternoon bike ride. They stay safe on the road by being careful and following rules. Sari doesn't ride too far ahead of Grandma. She just learned how to ride her bike, and staying close to Grandma helps her feel safe. They watch out for cars and look left and right before crossing any streets. They obey all of the street signs, just like the driver of a car does. Grandma is even teaching Sari special hand signals that bikers use to tell other bikers and drivers when they are stopping or turning.

Grandma has taught Sari that being safe is fun. Spending time together is even more fun! Sari couldn't ask for a better bike-riding partner.

Hiawatha Passing

By Jeff Hagan

On a cold starry night, a boy awoke in the upper reaches of his grandparents' tin-roofed farmhouse. Only moments before he'd fallen asleep, his harmonica at his side. Now he thought he'd heard a low, distant sound. Did it come from outside? He snuggled beneath his feather quilt, trying to figure it out.

This was the first time he'd spent the night at his grandparents' place, nestled way out in a land of rolling hills and faded red barns. Far below his window two silver rails stretched across a wide valley covered with a thin layer of new snow.

What was that sound? he wondered. It had come to him as a soft hum, like a gentle breath on his harmonica. *Was it a dream?*

He listened. Nothing.

Slowly he rolled to one side of the bed and blew a puff of warm air onto the window, melting a little spot on the frozen glass. He pressed his finger there, rubbing away the frost until he created a porthole. Then he peered deeply through the hole, searching for mystery ships in the night.

For an instant the boy caught sight of a glint on the frozen steel railroad tracks at the edge of the farmyard.

Now he heard it.

A high-pitched whistle cracked across the countryside like the snap of a bullwhip. The rails began to hum. He could almost imagine them turning color: changing from

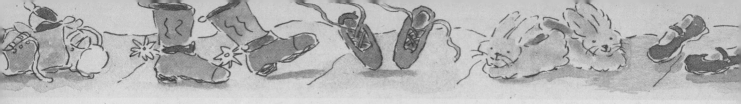

cold lifeless black to brilliant flame orange, throbbing with energy and promise.

Something big was approaching the farmhouse.

A single light shot through the darkness.

He could see a dark shadow behind it, swaying back and forth, spraying snow as it plowed down the valley.

The light thundered by the farmhouse, leading a huge steam engine. The earth trembled. The house shook.

The Hiawatha

A string of box-shaped lights flew by, roaring and rattling. Within each box was a blurred face peering out into the night: framed pictures of midnight travelers.

Who are these people? the boy wondered. *Where are they going? Why aren't they asleep under their feather quilts?*

Suddenly the last car whooshed by, its red taillight becoming smaller and smaller in the distance.

Little frost crystals spun and danced like toy tops until they came to rest on the frozen ground along the silver tracks. Silence returned to the valley.

The boy took one last look at the fleeting train, and at that instant a shooting star etched a brilliant trail across the velvet black sky.

Sleep overcame the boy. He was lucky; he was content. For on this night, at Grandma and Grandpa's farm, he had witnessed the passage of two shooting stars, one on earth and one in the heavens.

Man on the Moon

BY ANASTASIA SUEN

Moon, do you remember your first visitors? It was 1969 . . . Astronauts Collins, Aldrin, and Armstrong suited up. Each had flown in space, but no one had ever touched the moon. No one. Some said it couldn't be done. Astronauts Collins, Aldrin, and Armstrong were going to try.

Into *Apollo* 11 they climbed. The countdown began. 3–2–1 and . . . "Liftoff! Liftoff! *Apollo* 11 has cleared the tower!" *Saturn* 5 shot them into the sky. Around the Earth they flew as the rockets dropped off, then whoosh! straight for the moon. . . .

Hours and days passed. The people on Earth watched the astronauts on TV. Over and over the capsule turned. Suddenly, the sky went dark. It was the moon! For the first time, *Apollo* 11 saw the moon.

The astronauts circled, looking for a place to land. In the morning, their spacecraft would separate. *Columbia*, named after Columbus, would sail around the moon. The *Eagle*, like a bird, would fly there.

The next day, Aldrin and Armstrong climbed into the *Eagle*. Collins, in *Columbia*, pressed a button, and off the *Eagle* flew. . . . Buttons and gadgets, switches and lights! Alarms rang again and again. In the control room, Houston said, "Go." The *Eagle* flew on.

On the moon, craters loomed. The *Eagle* was going too fast! Armstrong took the controls and began to fly. Houston and the Earth waited.

Fifty feet
Thirty feet
Contact!

"Houston, Tranquility Base here. The *Eagle* has landed."
With cameras rolling, as millions watched, Astronaut Neil
Armstrong touched the moon. "That's one small step for man,"
he said, "one giant leap for mankind." Aldrin and Armstrong
took pictures, collected rocks, and planted the American
flag. Hours later, the *Eagle* left the moon and linked up
with *Columbia*.

Home again, Collins, Aldrin, and Armstrong splashed
down in the Pacific Ocean. Some said it couldn't be done.
Mike Collins, Buzz Aldrin, and Neil Armstrong proved them
wrong . . . and made history.

Read Aloud Anthology

Henry Hikes to Fitchburg

BY DONALD JOHNSON

One summer day, Henry and his friend decided to go to Fitchburg to see the country. "I'll walk," said Henry. "It's the fastest way to travel." "I'll work," Henry's friend said, "until I have the money to buy a ticket to ride the train to Fitchburg. We'll see who gets there first!"

His friend waved. "Enjoy your walk" he said.

Henry walked down the road to Fitchburg. "Enjoy your work," he called back.

Henry's friend filled the woodbox in Mrs. Alcott's kitchen. 10 cents.

Henry hopped from rock to rock across the Sudbury River.

His friend swept out the post office. 5 cents.

Henry carved a walking stick. 25 miles to Fitchburg.

Henry's friend pulled all the weeds in Mr. Hawthorne's garden. 15 cents.

Henry put ferns and flowers in a book and pressed them.

His friend painted the fence in front of the courthouse. 10 cents.

Henry walked on stone walls.

Henry's friend moved the bookcases in Mr. Emerson's study. 15 cents.

Henry climbed a tree. 18 miles to Fitchburg.

His friend carried water to the cows grazing on the grass in town. 5 cents.

Henry made a raft and paddled up the Nashua River.

Henry's friend cleaned out Mrs. Thoreau's chicken house. 10 cents.

Henry crossed a swamp and found a bird's nest in the grass. 12 miles to Fitchburg.

His friend carried flour from the mill to the village baker. 20 cents.

Henry found a honey tree.

Henry's friend ran to the train station to buy his ticket to Fitchburg. 90 cents.

Henry jumped into a pond. 7 miles to Fitchburg.

His friend sat on the train in a tangle of people.

Henry ate his way through a blackberry patch.

Henry's friend got off the train at Fitchburg Station just as the sun was setting.

Henry took a shortcut. 1 mile to Fitchburg.

His friend was sitting in the moonlight when Henry arrived. "The train was faster," he said.

Henry took a small pail from his pack. "I know," he smiled. "I stopped for blackberries."

House of Snow

BY RON FRIDELL

Did you ever build a snow fort for fun? Then you know what it's like to build a *pretend* house of snow. Now, do you know that some people build real snow houses? These snow houses are called igloos, and the people who live in them are called Inuits (IN-yoo-its).

The Inuit people used to be called Eskimos. They live way far north in Alaska, Canada, Greenland, and Russia. Some Inuits live very close to the North Pole. These are very cold places. In the winter, the ground is always covered in thick ice and hard snow. When most people build houses, they use bricks or wood. But the Inuit people use snow.

But not just any snow. Snow for an igloo must be tightly packed together and hard like a rock. The snow the Inuits use to build their igloos is so hard that they must cut it from the ground with a saw. They cut many blocks of snow, big blocks and little blocks. The big blocks are about two feet wide and three feet long.

Then they put the blocks together to make their igloo. Now, the place where you live probably has flat, square walls. Most homes have flat walls. So do most classrooms. But igloos don't have flat walls. Igloos have round, curved walls. They are shaped like a dome.

Do you know what a dome is? The bottom of a dome is flat, the top is round, and the sides all curve in toward the middle. If you cut an orange in half and set the two halves flat on a table, you would have two domes.

To make this igloo dome, the Inuits start with a row of snow blocks set in a circle. Then they add more rows to make the igloo higher and higher. Each new row also makes a smaller and smaller circle as the dome curves inward. At the very top, they leave a hole to let air in and out.

It would take many weeks or months to build the house you live in. But the Inuit people can build an igloo in just a few hours. How do they get into their snow house? They build a tunnel on one side. This tunnel helps keep the cold wind out. They can add a window too. They just cut a hole in the wall and fill it with a thin block of ice. This window lets in sunlight and gives the people inside a view of the outdoors.

The inside of an igloo is warmer than you might think. In fact, with just an oil lamp or two, the air gets warm, even toasty. And the bigger your family, the warmer it gets inside.

Imagine yourself and your family living in an igloo. You would keep your things on snow shelves cut into the wall. You would sit with your family and eat your meals on a raised platform of snow. And at night, you would all sleep on this platform, warm and safe from the cold winter night in your igloo. Would you like to live in a home made of snow?

The Elves and the Shoemaker

ADAPTED BY AMY EHRLICH

There was once a shoemaker who became poorer and poorer as the years went by. At last he had leather enough only for one pair of shoes. In the evening he cut out the pattern and then he went to sleep.

The next morning he took up a needle and thread, meaning to sew the shoes. But there they stood, neatly sewn and finished on his table. The shoemaker could not believe his eyes. Not a stitch was out of place and the work was better than any he had ever seen.

As he held the shoes, marveling at them, a customer entered the shop. He was so pleased with the shoes that he paid far more than the ordinary price, and the shoemaker was able to buy leather for two pairs more.

He cut them out in the evening, and the next morning prepared to begin work. But there was no need for it because the shoes had already been made and were as well stitched and handsome as the other pair. The first two customers who came into his shop bought them for a good price. And this time the shoemaker was able to buy leather enough for four pairs.

Early the next morning the four pairs of shoes were finished as before. And so it went. What the shoemaker cut out at night was finished in the morning, and customers were never lacking. Soon the shoemaker became a wealthy man.

From *The Random House Book of Fairy Tales*, adapted by Amy Ehrlich and illustrated by Diane Goode. Introduction by Bruno Bettelheim, copyright © 1985 by Amy Ehrlich. Illustration copyright © 1985 by Diane Goode. Introduction copyright © 1985 by Bruno Bettelheim. Used by permission of Random House Children's Books, a division of Random House, Inc.

Always he wondered about the skill of the work, and one evening he said to his wife, "How would it be if we were to sit up tonight to see who has been helping us these many months?"

She agreed at once and so they did not go to bed, but lit a candle and hid themselves in a corner of the room. Just at midnight two tiny little men came and sat down at the shoemaker's table. They immediately began to work. They stitched and hammered and sewed so neatly and quickly that the shoemaker was amazed. As soon as everything was finished and stood upon the table, they ran quickly away.

"The little men have made us rich and I think we ought to thank them," said the shoemaker's wife in the morning. "I shall sew them tiny shirts and pants and coats and knit them caps and socks. And you must make them each a pair of shoes."

The shoemaker and his wife worked hard all day and had everything ready by evening. Then they hid themselves to see how the little men would receive their presents.

At midnight the two came back into the room and sat down at the table. But instead of leather cut out and waiting, they found the wonderful little clothes.

First the little men were surprised and then they were delighted. They put on the shirts and pants, the coats and socks and caps, and they buckled the tiny shoes upon their feet. When they were done they ran their hands up and down the pretty clothes and admired each other, singing:

> "Now that we're boys so fine and neat,
> Why cobble more for others' feet?"

They hopped and danced about the shoemaker's shop, leaping over chairs and tables and then out the door. From this night on the two little men came back no more, but the shoemaker continued to do well as long as he lived and had good luck in all he attempted.

Robin's Nest

It was a cold, gray April day. Thomas stared at the puzzle he just put together. "I'm bored," he thought. He looked out at the cloudy sky and the new damp leaves blowing in the wind. It looked too dreary to play outside. Then a flash of color in the sky caught his eye.

Thomas ran to the window. He searched everywhere for that orange streak. There it was! A robin with dark orange feathers on his chest soared quickly through the sky and dove into the branches of a pine tree. Suddenly it flew back into the yard and hopped around the corner toward the porch. It came back seconds later with something long in its beak. "Is that string?" Thomas wondered.

Over and over the robin picked up something—string, a stem of grass, or twig—and took it to some secret hiding spot in the pine tree. Every time it flew back out, the robin's beak was empty. Thomas watched until lunchtime. "What could that robin be doing?" Thomas wondered.

Thomas was so excited to see what that robin was up to that he could barely eat his lunch. And he thought this day was going to be boring! Thomas raced outside to the pine tree and looked quickly for some clue of what the robin was up to. And there it was, just beyond Thomas's reach: a tiny round nest tucked snugly into the space where two branches grew together.

Thomas looked around for the robin, but it already saw him! The robin was perched on top of a bush watching him! Thomas sat down quietly and stayed very still. Soon, the robin got busy again. Back and forth, back and forth, the robin flew all afternoon.

Thomas sat, never taking his eyes off of the robin building its nest. Once, the robin returned with a stick. The stick was longer than the robin, and the busy bird kept dropping it. The stick was so big that the robin couldn't get it between the branches. The robin tried and tried, but the stick kept getting stuck. The robin finally dropped the stick.

From time to time, the robin flew to a little muddy puddle by the sidewalk. Thomas thought the bird was taking a drink. All that flying must make a little bird very thirsty. But as Thomas watched closely, he saw that the robin was scooping up mud! It returned to its nest and poked clumps of mud around the twigs and string to glue them together. The mud made the nest stronger!

Finally, the proud robin stood on the edge of the nest and sang a beautiful song. Soon another bird answered and flew to the nest from a nearby oak tree. Thomas knew that nests provide shelter for birds and that they lay eggs and raise their babies there. That means that soon a whole family will be living in Thomas's pine tree!

The two birds twittered sweet songs for a while. They poked their beaks here and there, pushing twigs and grass in place. Then the first robin hopped out onto the branch and flew toward Thomas. Thomas stayed very still. "What's happening?" he wondered. The bird gently landed on the cap beside him. It tried to pull a string out of the cap, but none would come. Then, to Thomas's surprise, the robin took hold of the brim of the cap and flew off! Using all its strength, it made it up to the nest with the red stocking cap. Thomas laughed. The cap had kept him warm during the winter. Now it would keep the baby birds warm in the spring!

Night in the Country

BY CYNTHIA RYLANT

There is no night so dark, so black as night in the country.

In little houses people lie sleeping and dreaming about daytime things, while outside—in the fields, and by the rivers, and deep in the trees—there is only night and nighttime things.

There are owls. Great owls with marble eyes who swoop among the trees and who are not afraid of night in the country. Night birds.

There are frogs. Night frogs who sing songs for you every night: reek reek reek reek. Night songs.

And if you are one of those people in one of those little houses, and if you cannot sleep, you will hear the sounds of night in the country all around you.

Outside, the dog's chain clinks as he gets up for a drink of water.

Far over the hill you hear someone open and close a creaking screen door. You wonder who is up so late.

And, if you lie very still, you may hear an apple fall from the tree in the back yard.

Listen: Pump!

Later, the rabbits will patter into your yard and eat pieces of your fallen apples. But only when they think you are asleep.

And all around you on a night in the country are the groans and thumps and squeaks that houses make when they are trying, like you, to sleep.

Outside . . . A raccoon mother licks her babies. A cow nuzzles her calf. An old pig rolls over in the barn.

And toward morning, one small bird will be the first to tell everyone that night in the country is nearly over.

The owls will go to sleep, the frogs will grow quiet, the rabbits will run away.

Then they will spend a day in the country listening to you.

A House By the Sea

BY JOANNE RYDER

If I could live in a little house,
I'd live in a house by the sea.
Some days I'd visit the frisky seals,
and some days they'd visit me.
We'd walk in the rain,
those seals and I,
till we'd stop for a slice
of fish-eyed pie.
When I got too wet,
or they got too dry,
we'd hug and we'd run
and we'd yell, "Good-bye."
I'd watch and I'd wave
to those seals in the sea,
and their flippers would splash,
waving back at me.
If I could live in a little house,
I'd live in a house by the sea.
And I'd whisper at night
when the moon was bright
"Would you please give a wish to me?"
And I'd wish I could fly
in the star-speckled sky
and wash my face in a cloud,

and I'd sing to the moon
a silly sea tune till he
laughed and laughed out loud.
Then I'd land on a whale
with a black-and-white tail
who would rock me fast asleep,
and she'd carry me home
on a crest of foam
over the waters deep.

If I could live in a little house,
I'd live in a house by the sea.
An octopus would live next door
and take good care of me.
With an arm doing this,
and an arm doing that,
he'd cook and make my bed.
He'd sweep the floor and paint my walls
and wash the clothes and answer calls
and bake me chocolate bread.
I'd read him stories
while he worked
and serve him seaweed tea,
and I would thank him very much
for taking care of me.

If I could live in a little house,
I'd live in a house by the sea.
Some days I'd catch the sea in a pail.
Some days the sea would catch me!
I'd be wet, wet, wet
from my nose to my toes,
bobbing away from the shore
till the sea changed its mind
and carried me back
and tossed me alongside my door.

When I can live in a little house,
I'll live by a house in the sea.
And I'll play in the sand,
dancing hand in hand
with a crab who is fond of me.
We'll play crab games
and trade our names,
so if you come calling me,
she'll hold out a claw
to shake your paw
as friendly as she can be.
Just ask the way
to the *crab* by the bay
and she'll point
the path to *me*.

Whenever you come
to the little house
that sits at the edge of the sea,
if you like, we can play
in the sand all day
a crab game, or two, or three.
And I'll call you, *Me,*
and you'll call me, *You,*
and no one will know
who is who
but us two
as we dance
round the rim
of the sea.

Animals' Houses

By James Reeves

Of animals' houses
    Two sorts are found—
Those which are square ones
    And those which are round.

Square is a hen-house,
    A kennel, a sty:
Cows have square houses
    And so have I.

A snail's shell is curly,
    A bird's nest round;
Rabbits have twisty burrows
    Underground.

But the fish in the bowl
    And the fish at sea—
Their houses are round
    As a house can be.

From *A Puffin Quartet of Poets.* Copyright © 1970 by James Reeves.
Reprinted by permission of Penguin Books.